Praise for Texting The Almighty

"As a counselor, I've helped people deal with life's problems, as well as working through my own. This can be very overwhelming. After reading <u>Texting The Almighty</u>, you will realize your place in the universe and the complete love that God has for you. You will understand that you have power over your own problems and your outlook on life. Once you understand that and have that security, then navigating through life's issues is more accessible."
    -Colleen Giuliana, LPC, owner, Harmony Health

"<u>Texting The Almighty</u> is a powerful masterpiece that allows you to see God and spirituality from a different perspective that enlightens our world as we know it. This includes biblical and scientific concepts and comparisons in a way that has not been previously done. I highly recommend this to both soul searchers just starting their journey, and those who have had this type of study as a life-long endeavor.
It is both informational and inspiring and I am a changed person after reading this wonderful book."
    -Laura Wagar, Reading Specialist and Special Education Teacher.

"As an R.N., I see the speed of a patient's recovery dependent to a great extent on a positive attitude and religious experience. This book, <u>Texting The Almighty</u>, offers the reader a new way of experiencing God. It may be foreign to your sense of traditional experience, or it may open up a new personal dialogue with the Almighty. Either way, it will provoke you and challenge you, both spiritually and intellectually, with the possibilities that are presented. Nice job, Dad!"
    -Jacqueline Faust, R.N., Crittenden Hospital, Rochester, MI

"Ken has written an insightful book for anyone who has ever wondered about God. As a believer, Ken explores his conception of God, and as he does, he allows us to explore our own. As a former math and science teacher, he uses mathematical and scientific examples to investigate the nature of God. There is something here for everyone from the atheist to the religious fundamentalist and everyone in between. All in all, <u>Texting The Almighty</u> is a good read on an important subject.
    -Dr. Edward Hill, Professor of Writing at WCC, MI

Texting The Almighty

Texting The Almighty

by

Ken Bartley

Chapbook Press

Schuler Books
2660 28th Street SE
Grand Rapids, MI 49512
(616) 942-7330
www.schulerbooks.com

ISBN 13: 9781943359332

Library of Congress Control Number: 2016958691

Copyright © 2016 Ken Bartley
All rights reserved.

No part of this book may be reproduced in any form without express permission of the copyright holder.

Printed in the United States by Chapbook Press.

This book is dedicated to

Carol

my wife of 54 years

Many thanks to

Ed Hill, Jim Will,

Paul Giuliana, and Scott Faust

for their help and guidance

Table of Contents

Foreword	13
Introduction	21
Chapter 1 Monday	27
Chapter 2 Tuesday	35
Chapter 3 Wednesday	53
Chapter 4 Thursday	81
Chapter 5 Friday	99
Chapter 6 Saturday	117
Chapter 7 Sunday	137
Finis	145
Appendix	149

Foreword

"An unexamined life is not worth living."
Socrates

Plato quotes Socrates in THE APOLOGY as making this statement at his trial in which he is condemned to death. Socrates is firmly saying that individuals need to examine their lives to decide what they believe, and how they should live their lives. At the heart of this examination for many people is the question of God. A person must decide what he or she thinks about God. Is there a God? Do I believe in God? What might be the nature of God?

Ken has written a wonderful book, TEXTING THE ALMIGHTY, in which he asks these questions and explores his relationship with God. Ken believes in God, and so the issue is not does God exist, but rather what is the nature of God, and what is God's relationship to human beings. As Ken explores his relationship with God, we have an opportunity to investigate our own relationship with God.

To explore this relationship, Ken creates a series of text-messages using his smart phone in which he has conversations with God over a seven day period. He begins by texting God and wondering if he will get a response. Surprisingly, he does. What follows is a dialogue between Ken and God in which God reveals His true nature to Ken.

Ken divides these dialogues into seven books. Book I sets the stage as Ken views God as a loving parent. God is someone we can talk to informally, conversationally about anything, and we will not be judged. And so in Book I, Ken asks God if they can talk about some questions regarding how God relates to human beings. God says certainly, and so the adventure begins.

Book II begins with God telling Ken to record these conversations so that people can comprehend what He is really like. Ken asks God why He simply can't make himself known to humans and take all the uncertainty about the existence of God out of life. God answers by saying that people must be free to make their own choices. God states that human existence is all about free will. People must decide for themselves whether or not to believe in Him. Every now-and-then, He will enter human history to tweak the system, but, for the most part, He lets people make their own decisions. God tells Ken that your choices determine who you are, and what kind of person you will become.

Ken follows by asking God about the Bible: is the Bible the word of God? God answers yes and no. He tells

Ken that He dictated the Bible to humans and sometimes they took liberties with what He had said. God never intended for His words to be used to justify war or things like the Inquisition. Some have used the Bible to enforce political control and have power over people. That is not right. The Bible is a book of faith, not of fact. Persons need to use their minds and think when they read the Bible. And this ends Book II.

Ken is a former math and physics teacher, and so much of Book III has a scientific slant to it. Ken and God discuss biological evolution and the beginning of creation. They discuss natural selection and survival of the fittest. God tells Ken that these early forms of life led to the creation of human beings that would be given a soul.

In Book III, God tells Ken that at birth, humans are given a chunk or quantum of spiritual substance: a soul. This quantum of spiritual substance leads humans to ask three profound questions: "Where did I come from?" "Why am I here?" "What is my destiny?"

God says to Ken that He will help humans deal with these questions if they will only ask for His help. This brings the reader to a very interesting section of the book: how God interacts with humans. God tells Ken that if humans are open to Him, He will help them by communicating with them through what may be compared to electromagnetic waves. This exchange between God and Ken ends Book III.

The fourth dimension and how God may interact with humans is the subject of Book IV. Ken begins by describing one, two and three dimensional worlds and then describes what a fourth dimensional world might be like. God tells Ken that there are more than four dimensions, but that He, God, often operates in the fourth dimension when dealing with humans. When persons die, their spiritual components pass into the fourth dimension. In this section, Ken talks about Dark Matter, Black Holes, and Einstein and the speed of light. Ken uses some pretty sophisticated math formulas to suggest how God relates to humans. This should appeal to the mathematically minded.

Books V begins with Ken describing Einstein's relativistic mass equation and relates this to a spiritual substance. Later in Book V, God again discusses how He communicates to humans through waves, but that many times our brains try to block these waves out. Because we want to be logical, we dismiss some of these thoughts from God as being ridiculous, resulting from an overworked imagination. At times, God may try to communicate with us through intuition, but men, especially, do not trust their feelings. Women are much better at trusting their intuition. God then tells Ken that persons can open themselves to Him through meditation, by spending time in nature, appreciating a work of art, listening to a symphony or reading a poem. Any of these activities need to be done quietly and reflectively. This ends Book V.

In Book VI, Ken and God talk, among other things, about the idea of hell. God tells Ken that there is no hell. God wants to help people, not punish them. God does not punish people; people punish themselves. After we die, we get to revisit our past lives and look at the impact that our decisions have had on other people. People who have lived terrible lives, like a Hitler or Stalin, must feel the pain, suffering, humiliation, and death that they have caused people. A person who has lived a wonderful life, like Abraham Lincoln, will experience the joy slaves felt when they were finally set free.

For good or for evil, persons will experience the good or the bad that they are responsible for. God tells Ken that the key to how we should live our lives is the Golden Rule. Treat others as you want to be treated. All of us are really one large family. We are all related as brothers and sisters, and we should treat each other as members of a loving family. This ends Book VI.

God tells Ken in Book VII that their time together is drawing to a close. Ken asks God what he should do with all that God has told him. Ken wonders if he should start a new church. God tells Ken to simply make people aware of the fact that they are all brothers and sisters. Treat others with respect and compassion. Life is a gift. Choose to enjoy it. Enjoy your family, your friends and the things that bring you joy. That is the message.

In the conclusion of the book, Ken states that he continues to grow and wishes the best for his readers.

Ken offers ideas about God that will appeal to a wide range of people. For atheists and agnostics, he may convince them to revisit some of their positions. For religious fundamentalists, he may cause them to rethink some of their positions. For many of us simply asking some basic questions about God, he has given us much to think about and a lot of hope.

I have known Ken for over sixty years and so have heard him talk about many of these ideas. I can say that Ken sincerely means what he discusses in his book. My hope is that you enjoy this book as much as I have.

Dr. Edward Hill

Introduction

Do you remember the old elephant jokes? You may not, as they were popular back in the 1960's, when I was in college. So if you don't remember them, let me enlighten you. The jokes were usually in the form of a riddle; some of them were really dumb and most of them were absurd, but they often made you laugh for one reason or another. Here are a few that I recall:

Q: What do you call an elephant that rides a bus?
A: A passenger.

Q: How do you stop a charging elephant?
A: Take away his credit card!

And my favorite:
Q: Where does an elephant sit?
A: Anywhere he chooses.

And with a slight change, that last one provides a basis for the beginning of this book:

Q: How does God choose to relate to human beings?

A: Any way He chooses!

And people have opened up various ways of confronting God. They have kept Him in a box (the arc of the covenant). They have put Him into statues and then bowed down before them. They have identified Him in nature and sought Him out by being in or living there. They have kept Him in a chalice on the altar and only the priest had access; you had to stay by your seats on your knees.

This book seeks to answer the question: Is it possible that God could relate to people in an informal way, engaging in casual conversation, and "hanging out" in a friendly environment?

I'm sure your first reaction is "No! God is holy and unapproachable. The only thing that we can hope for is to bow down and hope that he doesn't slap us because we're such terrible people." And it appears that He honors our wishes, as He lets people do all of the above.

It may be that He takes whatever He can get; any relationship with us is better than nothing. But it also may be that He's just waiting for someone to take the step of communicating with Him in a relaxed and informal manner. Then that someone will spread the word and a new era of spiritual experience will be ushered in.

Hopefully, this book will provide that step.

But anyone can make a statement and say, "this is the way things work!" I have tried to avoid that and have attempted to support many ideas with math or science. I have assumed that the reader needs simple, detailed information with many of these concepts and hope that you will find it easy to understand. If your background is of a more advanced nature, then just skip down to the next paragraph and continue your read.

Although much of the information appears to need a footnote, I assure you that all the ideas were pulled from the recesses of my memory which were established from an extensive study of math and physics and almost 50 years of teaching these subjects. Biblical locations are cited with verses whenever they are mentioned and there is only one time when a footnote might be needed: the notes about passengers on the planes on 9/11 was taken from Dr Larry Dossey's book, The Power of Premonitions

Although this book is listed as fiction, the ideas and statements presented during all the texting are felt to be true. They were revelations from God using the techniques and methods revealed in this book. Hopefully, you will be able to apply these ideas to your life and they will enable you to enjoy a more relaxed and fulfilling relationship with the Almighty. Enjoy the read!

Chapter 1 - Monday

The events which occurred in the few days of last month now seem distant and surreal, yet their impact has been profound. When I think back on those experiences, I cannot believe that they actually happened; they seem impossible and unbelievable. Yet everything that happened, though impossible to verify directly, now forms the basis, for me, of a new paradigm for the way things are and how they should be. These experiences have transformed the way I understand life and the world and have shaken up my religious beliefs tremendously; but they have fortified my faith in a way that I have never experienced before.

But you be the judge. Read my accounts and see for yourself if the revelations that were given to me seem reasonable and real. Should they be the foundation of a new attitude if this world and its people are to survive? Should they replace the old school of thought which has determined the way things have been done for so long? With the animosity among religions at an all-time high, there has to be a new way of viewing the world and its people and their religious philosophies. There must be an understanding and a sense of caring among individuals and cultures that will let all people live a life without want and have an opportunity for happiness. I believe that I have been given insight into the way in which that can actually come about.

    My experience actually started out quite innocently on a Monday morning. I'm a retired math and science teacher and one of the best things about retirement is not having to wake up to an alarm. And after I do get up, I am able to spend about 2 hours drinking coffee and playing, um, I mean working with my new friend, the smart phone.

    For years, I resisted the purchase of a cell-phone. I originally had a bag phone which, although more powerful than its hand held cousin, was cumbersome and using it was difficult. Then I got a plain old cell phone, which I used for calling and a little texting, but not much more. Finally, with coaxing from my family, I gave in and got one with all its bells and whistles. With the little icons on the screen, which you would touch in order to summon the application, it seemed almost like magic. Who knew that stroking glass could produce so many amazing feats?

    One of the neatest things was texting. You would

type in messages to someone, and they would stay on the right side of the screen, and the responses from that person would stay on the left side; you could actually keep track of conversations over a period of time. It was really neat, and I did a lot of it. It was a way to stay in touch with people without actually having to talk to them. You could call them if you wanted to talk to them for a while, but for a short comment or question, texting was the way to go. And you could think about what to say and how to say it and not have to respond immediately to a question that a person might ask you over the phone.

 But texting the Almighty hit me slowly. I was pondering the way prayer was practiced in today's churches and thinking about what it must be like from God's point of view. If the relationship between God and a person is like that of a parent and child, then the way prayer is carried out in a formal setting is crazy. Imagine your child coming into your room and bowing down before you and uttering the words, "Oh father, who art perfect and all-powerful and doest bestow all of life's blessings upon me." You would look puzzled and say "What the heck are you doing. . . Get up and let's throw the ball around.". And if he persisted, you would continue, "You don't have to thank me for all the stuff I do for you. . . It's what a father does for his son.

I love doing it; now let's go play ball."

I began to wonder if talking with God could be that informal and relaxed. It all depends on the kind of God in which you believe. If you believe that God is angry with you all the time, then you've got to appease Him and convince Him to be nice to you even though He thinks you're a terrible person. You do this by bowing down and mumbling all kinds of memorized prayers which will convince Him that you should receive His mercy and blessings. And this all-powerful, all-knowing, omnipotent Deity will then be convinced that you are sincere and well-meaning and not see through your facade; He will then be nice to you and help you with life's demands. There's something wrong with that picture; it sounds like the image of God perpetuated by the priests and ministers and designed to keep people in line and getting them to give money, rather than providing open communication with the Almighty. If your God is going to slap you every time you do something 'bad', then you're going to enter his presence with fear and you will bow down and hope you'll not be killed if He gets upset with you. I was trained to believe in this type of God, and the phrase "the fear of God" was mentioned often in the church settings in which I was raised.

But imagine if God were loving and understanding ALL of the time, even when your behavior was off the wall. Imagine that you could share with Him any thought or secret or idea and know that He would understand, that there would be no rejection nor punishment, and you could continue in this intimate relationship with the creator of the universe uninterrupted by fear or guilt.

I began to embrace this new image of God and started to mutter prayers under my breath using phrases like "Good morning God", "Wow... Great sunset, Lord", and "Man, that burger was fantastic.. Thanks!" And often I would get responses from Him, at least I thought they were. Thoughts would pop into my head that could be construed as coming from God; often they were feelings of peace and awareness. This new belief began to replace my former feelings of fear and worry as I slowly began to have new confidence in our relationship.

With this new attitude and a new cell phone, it was only natural that I should wonder if I could actually text the Almighty. I began typing in some possible numbers, none of which worked.

Then I tried the number 7154. It came from taking the number in the alphabet for each letter in the word GOD. G is the 7th letter O the 15th and D the 4th. It was a good idea but still nothing. When I text the TV company to get a pay-per-view movie, I use 6 numbers so I knew I needed something with 6 numbers.

I started trying other words and numbers but the thought that in order to get GOD, you ought to text GOD, made me feel that perhaps I should use the word GOD in another language. I tried GOTT, which is GOD in German. But G is 7, O is 15, T is 20, so the number to text is 7152020; that's 7 letters. I kept looking.

I then tried DIOS, which is GOD in Spanish. D is 4, I is 9, O is 15, and S is 19; that's 491519... yeah... 6 letters. I typed it in and texted:

Are you there, God?

And to my amazement, I got back

Yes. I am.
    Yah, right. It could be anyone and I was skeptical. I wrote

Who is "I am"

The response was amazing.

"I am that I am"

This is the response that Moses got from the burning bush on Mt. Sinai. Now the "I am" might have triggered that response from a biblical scholar but from the average hacker, I don't think so. Had I really contacted the Almighty? Another test was in order.

Is this God?

Yep.

How can I be sure?

Well, you've got a dentist appointment in 20 minutes, and we can text some more when you're done.

    I glanced at my notebook on the disk, and there it was in black and white. I began to glance around the room for hidden cameras or microphones that someone could use to watch or listen to me but of course saw nothing.

    Another possibility was that a person could have looked over the shoulder of the dental receptionist and made note of my appointment. Of course, how would that person have known I would be texting and then set up things at that number? It was crazy.

    This was the start of an amazing week that would revolutionize everything about the way I view the physical universe, my religious philosophy, and my attitudes about life and death and purpose. It would be a life-changing experience.

Chapter 2 - Tuesday

I typed in the number again and began to text, wondering if yesterday's experience was just a fluke.

> You there, God?

Yep.

It was an immediate response, like He was there, waiting for me. A hacker wouldn't do that nor have that capability, but I was still skeptical. I mean. . . texting my creator and exchanging ideas with Him or Her. It was a strange experience. I continued typing.

> I'm still wondering how you are able to do all this texting with me.

Hey, I'm God. I can run things the way I want, and right now, this is something I'd like to try.

> My vision of you and the way you work does not involve texting like this.

This is not the way I usually do things. My impact on humanity has usually been to interact through prayer requests and occasionally tweak the system when needed.

> So why the texting?

Because occasionally people need
to be set straight and reminded of
Spiritual values, so make sure and
write about your experiences with
Me so others will know what I'm
really like. Remember Jesus?
He was trying to redirect the
people and the Pharisees to a
more spiritual and less legalistic
way of getting to know Me.

> But they killed him!

Yep. So when you read some of the things
I'm going to tell you, expect great
controversy when you try to share them
with others.

> What new ideas shall I try to
> write about?

There are some new ideas, but many are
just new ways of looking at old ideas.
For example, creation; many believe
that I took only 6 days to create
everything, but that's wrong. I used
evolution. It's a great way to run creation.
You make the rules, sometimes called
physical laws, tweak the system to cause
The Big Bang, then sit back and watch things
happen.

> And then it runs smoothly to

>produce suns, planets, galaxies, life, animals, people, and everything that is here now?

Yep. Except every once in a while, you have to tweak the system if things need direction.

>You used "tweak" before. What do you mean by that?

That's where I impact your physical world in a manner which is undetectable and does not violate any of the known laws which I made up. It's really simple though. Quantum Mechanics has lots of room for messing with things and not be observed.

>Why do you have to be undetected? Why don't just let your presence be observed by people; it would prove your existence. And if you clobbered the bad guys, you could end suffering.

As soon as I show up, it's a different ball game. When the playwright comes on stage, the play's over and a completely new reality sets in. You can't have personal freedom or free will and yet live in a God dominated utopia.

> But there have been times when more than a 'tweak' was needed. 6 million Jews died in the holocaust; couldn't You have done more.

That actually was a case of my interfering more than usual; had I not, then 10 million Jews would have died and Hitler would have won the war. I actually thought somebody would spot Me when Hitler stopped bombing England and then invaded Russia.

> But wouldn't it be good to make your existence more obvious. It's impossible to 'prove' that You exist so people live with a lot of uncertainty?

Free Will . . . It's all Free Will. People have to decide for themselves how to live and whether or not to believe in Me. Your choices determine who you are and what kind of person you will become.

> But don't you get angry at people who don't believe in

> You and punish them after they die?

Please... I'd be a nasty Deity if I punished people for using their Me-given brain to conclude that I don't exist. Won't they be surprised when they get here? Things will work out eventually, but everyone's got to live their lives before they go on to the next level.

> So there's no hell?

Hell is a terrible concept! What kind of God would give you a brain and when you used it to reject a certain idea would then torture you and inflict on you unimaginable pain and suffering not for a year, nor for a decade, nor a century, but FOREVER? That's downright sadistic. That's not the work of a loving God.

> So, if You didn't initiate that idea, where did it come from?

Dante wrote his best-seller, Inferno, and the church saw that fear was a really good way to keep people In line. And when you have the power to "excommunicate", that's the ultimate control. It sure kept the offering plates full; and It still does.

> So, if I get some of these ideas out there, do you think that people will read and understand?

Some will but many will not. People get comfortable with their established beliefs and don't like new ideas rocking the boat. Besides, if it's not in the Bible, they'll reject it immediately.

> But the Bible is supposed to be your book, isn't it? A book without error? That's what the fundamentalists say.

A couple things here. You should know that it is my book, and I dictated a lot of Ideas right to the prophet or writer. The problem was that the writer often took my ideas and messed with them.

> Do you have some examples?

Yes. When a people wants to go war to secure new territory, then a religious fervor is an excellent way to fire up soldiers to risk their lives for their political leaders. So change a verse or 2 and quote me as saying that war is good to secure land, the promised land, and you can convince the people that I am the One that wants them to go to war. Then they get on the band wagon and are willing to die for Me. And it can get especially nasty when people use these ideas as an excuse to kill women and children. I would NEVER tell anyone to do that. That's terrible!

> When I read that in the old testament, I didn't think that sounded like You.

For sure!

> And there are some verses that show You being in favor of slavery.

When I told the writer of Exodus that I was definitely opposed to slavery. He thought, "but I want slaves so that can't be right." Not only did he change my message, he made up rules in My Name for how slavery should work, some of them pretty mean too. Check Exodus 21.

> I went to Exodus 21 and read it. It's got some nasty things that it says about how to treat slaves and attributes them to God.

> It sounds like Your desire for a relationship with man started out with a lot of problems.

Yes. When I made known to the priests who were building the temple in Jerusalem that I wanted to be close to and have a relationship with all the people, they said, "that ain't right! Only we are holy enough to enter into God's presence. We represent the church and only we can know God's Will. We'll find it out and tell the people what to do."
Talk about control.

> It sounds like a lot of Your message in its truest form is missing.

Right! And some times, guys just made up stuff and put it in the Bible if it suited their purpose. You've got to be very critical as you read.

> So you're saying that there are errors in the Bible?

People should realize that the Bible is a book of faith, not a book of fact. There are statements which are just plain wrong, and then there are cases where two statements about the same thing conflict or contradict each other.

> Example?

Tell me how the animals went onto Noah's arc.

> That's easy; 2 of every sort.

So look up Genesis 6:20 and then Genesis 7:2   I'll wait.

That's another neat thing about the smart phone: aps, little programs that do neat things for you, and one of my aps is the Bible. I looked up both passages and sure enough, Genesis 6:20 said the animals came to the arc 2 by 2. Then I checked Genesis 7:2 and there it said they came 7 by 7. Since it can't be both, I guess we can call it an error. I guess you could say that the writer of the 2 by 2 didn't notice the other 5 in line next to the 2, but any way you look at it, they are conflicting statements. I texted back:

> I never noticed that.

Not many do. People don't usually actually read the Bible; they just take another person's word for it. Another question: who was created first, man or the animals.

> I knew this one too, or thought I did. In Genesis 1, you rested on the 7th day, having made man on the sixth just AFTER the animals

OK, now read Genesis 2:19. The animals are being created AFTER Adam, and he is being called upon to give them names. So which is It? The point is that the author wasn't A scientist and didn't understand Evolution. He was correct in Stating that I was responsible for the Creation but thought I did it in a big poof which took 6 days, not the big bang, which took billions of years.

> How about errors in the new testament?

Remember the baptism of Jesus?

> John the Baptist was the guy that did the deed, right?

Yes. And when it was over the Holy Spirit came down and said something.

> He said "You are my beloved Son, in whom I am well pleased."

Yes. That was in the gospel of Mark.
But in the gospel of Matthew, it says
that the Holy Spirit said, "THIS is my
beloved Son, in whom I am well
pleased."

                        Isn't that the same thing.

Almost. It depends on whether I'm
speaking quietly to Jesus or to the
crowd which is watching the whole
thing.

                        I guess that's different.

Sure. It's speaking quietly to
Jesus or talking to the crowd.

                        Why the difference?

Matthew changed it because he's
writing for the Jews. He wants the
Jews to know that Jesus is the
Messiah that they've been waiting
for, and the best way to do that is
to have it announced to a group
of observers. Book of faith, not fact.

                        Any others?

Sure. And is it any wonder?
The gospels weren't even written
until 40 years after Jesus'
crucifixion. You can't even
remember where you put your

keys (LOL). So do you think the authors might get a few things wrong? Book of faith, not fact!

> I'm 76 and He is right. I'm glad we can both laugh about it. Of course, what am I going to say if I don't like it?

> What's another error?

How did Judas die?

> That was another easy one, or so I thought.

> > That's easy, he hanged himself. And all the gospels agree on this, at least the ones which contain the account.

Correct, but now read Acts 1:16-18

> I looked it up on my phone, and it was about Judas buying a field and "falling headlong, he burst asunder in the midst, and all his bowels gushed out." Wow, that's gross; I don't think I want to know all the details, but it's really nasty. But it's definitely not hanging. That's another contradiction.

> > I see what you mean. What about holy books of other

religions? Are there errors in all of them?

Sure, but because of your Christian background, let's just talk about the Bible. Besides, in some other religions, there are groups of fundamentalists who will try and kill you if you even imply that there may be any little item which is not quite accurate. And they claim that I'm the one that wants them to do the killing. That's terrible. I would never tell anyone to kill someone else just because they don't believe the same way.

I agreed and knew exactly what He was talking about. I was thinking about asking for divine intervention, but I knew the response would be "no dice. . . free will!" But the following text did come through:

I will provide guidance like I would for anyone when asked. I won't do the whole thing but together you and I can get through all kinds of difficulties.

I was wondering if there were errors in cases of faith rather than "fact" so I texted:

> It seems that the Bible has factual errors but are there errors in areas of faith. Isn't the area of faith more "absolute"?

In general, yes. There are many stories and parables about the way people ought to behave. The parable of the "Good Samaritan" is a story of the way everyone ought to treat their neighbor (which is everyone with whom a person comes in contact). And there's the story of Joseph being sold into slavery by his brothers and then forgiving them when they come to Egypt during a famine. Those are definitely ways that people should behave.

> So, the behavior of biblical characters is the way we ought to behave?

In general, yes. But you should still scrutinize all aspects of the individual's behavior. For instance, after Sodom and Gomorrah was destroyed, Lot's daughters decided to sleep with their father. That's not an example of good moral behavior.

> It sounds like you should read the Bible with a critical eye regardless of what type of guidance you are seeking.

In general, I would agree. Don't take anything for granted. Analyze everything connected with a moral precept.

> So evil can be present in situations which might not seem so?

There have been a huge number of nasty things done in the name of religion. The Inquisition and witch trials are just 2 events which illustrate the terrible things which can be done to innocent people by religious leaders. The church okay-ed torture to drive the devil out of a person... ridiculous.

> Ridiculous about the torture or the devil?

Both. Torture is never OK especially when condoned by a church. And when you want someone to blame for your guilt or fear, what better way than conjuring up a red guy with horns and a forked tail. It's actually quite a humorous image if it weren't for the terrible things that the delusion has spawned.

So... no devil?

Nope. It's nice to have something or someone to blame for all the things you're afraid of or feeling guilty about. Remember the comedian's comment, "The devil made me do it!". And the devil's also the CEO of Hell. Nice arrangement, eh?

So, the devil is not responsible for evil in the world.

Nope. If there were a devil, you'd have to explain where he came from and it's either from Me or evolution and neither makes sense... well actually evolution does but not in a conventional sense.

What do you mean?

Imagine that a high school acquaintance had beat the snot out of you years ago. Then, recently, you meet him again and the old memories surface. The animal instinct

to be top dog and extract
vengeance coupled with
those old memories and
you're tempted to key his
car, steal his laptop, or nudge
him off the curb as a car
passes. Your spirit urges
forgiveness and reconciliation,
thus the old image of an angel
on one shoulder and the
devil on the other.

         I get it.

Good. Occasionally, certain
behavior must be met with an
aggressive response, but, in
general, the solution should
emphasize the spiritual.

         Do you have examples of
         that?

Sure. Hitler had to be stopped
during WWII, and it didn't look
like slaves were going to be liberated
in any way except the Civil War.

         Both events were terrible!

You're right. But defeating evil
sometimes demands that kind of
solution if there's no other way.
Listen, we've covered a lot today,
let's wrap it up until tomorrow.
Besides your neighbor is at your door.

Sure enough, as soon as He texted that, I heard a knock at the door. I think He likes doing that. I texted that I would contact Him tomorrow. What an amazing experience this has been.

Chapter 3 – Wednesday

I woke with great anticipation of the day's possibilities. Imagine... texting God Himself, hanging out with Him, and my learning new things which I never imagined. What a wonderful thing to be able to do. I grabbed the phone and began again:

> You there Lord?

Of course.

> Yesterday, You were talking about the nature of evil and what evolution has to do with it.

First of all, we're talking biological evolution, not stellar evolution.

> I understand.

I knew that stellar evolution had to do with how stars develop from clouds of hydrogen. These hydrogen clouds then contract under gravity until they become so dense and the pressure in the inner core becomes so great that a nuclear reaction begins which changes hydrogen to helium and in the process generates immense energy. The star then burns for billions of years and goes through many changes (evolves) until it gets to the end of its life. Depending on how much mass the star has, it may end up as a black hole. As the internal pressure lessens in a massive star, gravity then causes the stars' mass to collapse in on itself. When billions of tons of mass collapse down into the size of a marble, then the gravitational field is so strong that nothing can escape from it, not even light, thus, the name, black hole. How's that for a 1 minute course in stellar evolution. For a more detailed explanation you can read one of the many books out there or watch some of the excellent TV shows that are available.

But biological evolution takes place after the planets form and cool, and the oceans are somewhat stable and able to support life. When the right combination and configuration of atoms and molecules are present with the right amount of energy, then life could form.

Did You have to "tweak" the system for life to begin?

Yes, I did. That first step is so complex
that random processes couldn't
put everything into a configuration
where life could begin by itself.
Once that first step occurred, then
things could move along on their
own. It was just a matter of time,

lots of it, until the stage was set for the establishment of the human species.

I understood the 2 parts of evolution: the first was natural selection, by which a new trait for the organism was introduced (which we now understand as the combination of the RNA from both parents into a new DNA which results into a potentially new trait for the offspring). And then it was the "survival of the fittest." If the new trait gave the organism an advantage for its survival, then it would indeed survive; if it did not, then it would die out. That's evolution; a wonderful mechanism responsible for the way things are now, along with a little 'tweaking".

So once life began, evolution took over and the various species developed over the millions and millions of years which took us to the place where humans were ready for "self-awareness," right?

You got it! And in the course of this development, I had to tweak the system once again to produce the eukaryotic cell structure with its nucleus and mitochondria, which then set the stage for more complex plants and animals.

Then, of course, there were the
dinosaurs and other situations
that had to be solved for humans
to begin developing, but
eventually, things were ready for a
human being with a soul.

> So the human being is
> now ready for a soul and
> it only took billions of
> years,

Hey, that's the way it works!
Life has developed from
a small microbe to a complex animal
with an unbelievable brain, and is
now ready for a spirit, which will
separate him from the rest of the
animals in a very unique way.

> So the spiritual aspect of
> man is what makes him
> different from the rest.

Yep. When a person is born, that
person is given a chunk or quantum
of spiritual substance that is the
soul.

> So the amount of spiritual
> matter given to an
> individual is quantized?

If quantum mechanics is good in
in the physical universe, then it
can work in the realm of the spirit

too. Plus, it's hard to have one and a half of you; it's one chunk for one person.

      Then physics here is good there?

In this case, sure, but you have to realize that you don't have all the equations and constants. You can't always start plugging spiritual values into physical equations to get predictions that make sense.

      But you can measure how much spiritual matter is in a 'soul'?

Yes, but you have to have the proper units. The amount of spiritual substance is measured in i-kg.

      I recognize the kg as kilograms, but I don't know what the "i" is doing there.

You've taught math, so you should know what "i" is.

   And I did. I recognized the "i" as the imaginary number

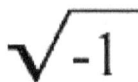

and kg. as the abbreviation for kilograms, the metric unit of measurement of the mass of an object. For our discussion, think of mass as weight, or how heavy an object is. One kilogram is equal to 2.2 pounds in our English system. That should be a more familiar idea than the imaginary number, "i", which I hope to explain to you in the next few paragraphs.

"i" is a number which is different from the usual numbers which can be expressed as whole numbers or fractions or decimals. If you put -1 into your calculator, and press the square root button, it will give you an error message. Go ahead and try it. You'll see.

If you understand what "i" is all about, then skip a couple of pages. If you don't, then follow me through on this. And if you hated math or were afraid of it, please give it a try; you may be pleasantly surprised.

Squaring a number means multiplying it by itself. So 2 squared is 2x2 which equals 4 and 5 squared is 5x5=25. It's written like this: $2^2=4$ and $5^2=25$. Easy so far, eh?

But it works for negative numbers too. You may

not think that you're familiar with negative numbers, but if you think about it, you'll find that you are. Temperatures below zero are negative. If the temperature is 20 below, it is -20. when the Dow loses 8 points, that's -8. If you owe someone $10 that's -10. And if you have $10 in your wallet, but owe someone else $10, you could write ($10) + (-$10) = 0 or (10) + (-10) = 0 which would represent the total that you have. I put the numbers in parentheses to keep them separated from each other.

But we want to see what you get when you square a negative and the truth is that Negative times Negative gives you a Positive answer. If that seems strange to you, then let me give you an example using the English language.

If you wanted somebody to do something, then you would say, "DO THAT," and when it is done, it's a positive result. If you say, "<u>DO</u> <u>NOT DO</u> THAT," then it doesn't happen, and that's a negative result.

But now, when you say, "<u>DON'T</u> <u>NOT DO</u> THAT," it means you will refrain from "not doing" something; this means that it will get done, a positive result. , i.e. negative times negative yields positive, and this is what this example was leading up to. One more time:

Negative X Negative = Positive

Here's an example using money. When you earn money,

that's a positive number in your budget. When you pay a bill, that's negative. When either of those occurs individually, for so many months, that number would be positive; when either of those does not happen for a number of months, that would be negative.

If you made $200 for 3 months, you would be ahead by $600 or (+$200) x (+3) = +$600,

If you had to pay out $100 for each of 2 months, you would be out by $200 or (-$100) X (+2 months) = -$200. The negative sign means that you're out that amount.

If you don't make your $200 for each of 3 months, then you would be out $600 or ($200) X (-3) = -$600 The negative sign means that you're out that amount.

And finally, if you don't have to pay out $100 for each of 3 months, you are ahead by $300 or (-$100) X (-3) = +$300 and this last example is the one which I want to emphasize: a negative number times another negative number equals a positive number.

This is what the last few paragraphs have been shooting for. I hope it didn't scare you off and that you either refreshed your memory or else gave you a new experience in using math. If I went too fast, then go back over it and this time read it a little slower and think about each step as it happens.

Squaring a number means "multiply the number by itself." Squaring a negative number must give a positive answer. $(-3)^2 = (-3) \times (-3) = +9$ and $(-4)^2 = (-4) \times (-4) = +16$. If you've got this then we're ready for the square root.,

Every math operation has its opposite: the opposite of adding is subtracting, and the opposite of multiplying is dividing. And there must be an opposite to squaring a number; that is where the square root comes in. It works like this: if you want to take the square root of 36, you ask yourself, "what number times ITSELF is equal to 36?" And in this case, the answer is 6. But that's not the only number which, when multiplied by itself, gives 36. We have just been through great lengths to show that $(-6) \times (-6)$ is also 36 so the answer is not only +6; it is also -6. It turns out that every time you take a square root, you get 2 answers, one positive and one negative. So $\sqrt{36} = 6$ and -6.

Another example is the following: $\sqrt{100}$ means the square root of 100. Its value is 10, but it's also -10. This is because $(10)^2 = (10) \times (10) = 100$ and $(-10)^2 = (-10) \times (-10) = 100$.

Now for the crazy part: what is the square root of -49? That's right, what is the square root of a negative number. Remember that the only way to get a negative answer for a multiplication problem is by multiplying a negative by a positive and when you are taking a square root, you are asking what number times ITSELF gives you -49. THERE IS NO ANSWER. Go ahead and put -49 into your calculator and hit the square root button. Yes, it says error. This prompts the question "what can be done when you confront a situation like this?"

The way you do it is to split -49 into (-1)x49 and then take the square root of each part. The square root of 49 = 7 and you're left with $\sqrt{-1}$. So what do you do then? Well, you take this new number, which is not like any other number you've ever dealt with, and you give it a name. You call the square root of -1 = i, which is what mathematicians have been calling it since the 17th century. So the answer for $\sqrt{-49}$ = 7i and -7i

"i" is a number which does not exist in the set of real numbers and mathematicians actually call this an imaginary number. It's used in higher mathematics, but often, when working on a problem and getting some answer with "i" in it, they say that there is no solution to the problem. It's almost mystical; you have a number which you have produced, yet which has no meaning in the physical world when coupled with kilograms. Yet now we find out that it can be used in conjunction with the spirit and the soul. I went back to my texting.

> I do know what "i" is but I always used it as an imaginary number, not as a unit. Are kilograms the same for measuring the mass of an object and the mass of spiritual substance.

Not at all. Even though kg is used in the new unit, an i-kg is completely different from regular mass and is used in calculations with spiritual quantities.

> It doesn't seem right that numbers should be used with spiritual matters. Spiritual matters should have a certain "holiness" associated with them.

I understand your reticence, but think about it; you don't get upset when a number is used to describe your weight or height. And the wonder you have when seeing a beautiful rainbow is not diminished by a discussion of the wavelengths of light or refraction of light inside a raindrop, at least it shouldn't.

> I realize that, but the amount of spiritual matter in a soul is a new idea and a bit difficult to take in.

You'll get used to it when you work with the new ideas for a while. Think of the 2 basic quantities in nature: mass and electric charge. Each has a force field associated with it. The force field from a mass is gravity and that of an electric charge is an electric field.

> Is there a field associated with a spiritual body?

Sure. Some people call it an aura.

> I've heard of that. Wow! These are really new ideas.

Yes! But think about it. A soul introduced into a body/brain which has evolved over millions of years must blend with the animal portion in order to function as a complete human being capable of intimacy, love, concern, creativity, compassion, and many other traits which are impossible in an animal which does not possess a spiritual component.

> Is this where self-awareness occurs?

Yes. The introduction of spirit into the human animal provokes the 3 big questions: "Where did I come from?", 'Why am I here?", and "What is my destiny?" And that last one has to with death and beyond.

> But if a person doesn't believe in You, then the answers to those questions are: evolution, reason, and oblivion. That's a pretty empty life if you don't believe.

It can be. But there are so many things in life which provide meaning: love and family and friends, the beauty of the earth, music and art, ideas and philosophy. All involve the spiritual aspect of life; the atheists just don't believe it.

> And you've said it doesn't matter whether people acknowledge you or not.

In some cases, the atheists are better than religious people.

> How can that be?

Think about a loving deed that a

person does, like helping someone
pick up groceries which have been
dropped. If the helping person is
religious, the deed might have been
done out of fear that I might be
angry if that person had not helped.
And you don't want to get Me angry!
At least that's their worry.

> And the atheist?

If the atheist helps, then it's out of
that person's love and kindness; that's
a lot better motivation than fear and
it says a lot about their character.

> So You don't
> care if an atheist
> believes in you or not?

It's better for them if they do. Their
spiritual growth can occur without
my obvious presence, but if they tap
onto my power, then it's to their
benefit.

> So you will help everyone,
> regardless if they believe in
> You or not?

Yes, but only help for spiritually
positive things; I'm not going to
help you steal money or hurt people.
And it's not a quid pro quo set-up
where I'll help you only if you do

something for me. That reeks of the animal component. But if you do believe in Me, then you'll be more open to my guidance. And you have to realize that I'm there for you and you must not be afraid of Me; I'm not out to hammer you if you step out of line. Fear, guilt, and anger are three of the things which will make you stay an arm's length away from Me.

> But how do you guide us if You won't step into our world in a physical sense?

Guidance involves communication from me to you. I know you understand how particles with an electric charge, like electrons, produce electromagnetic waves.

> Yes.

And I did. I knew that atoms are made of electrons around a nucleus. The electrons have a negative electric charge and move around the nucleus, which has a positive charge, due to the protons there. There are also neutrons there, which interact with the protons to hold the nucleus together. The electric attraction between the negative electrons and the positive protons hold the atom together. In a metal, the electrons can move around and when they move up and down a long wire (an antenna), they produce radio waves.

There are many kinds of waves, and, I'll bet you're most familiar with water waves because you have seen them before. You might have seen them from a boat or while sitting on a dock; either way, you probably noticed some interesting things about them. Here are some things which you might have observed, referring to the diagram below:

As the wave passes by, you would notice that there are high points followed by low points. The high point is called a peak and the low point a trough. The distance between 2 peaks is called the wavelength, and if you count the number of waves which pass you in a certain time, you have the frequency. The speed or velocity of a wave may be calculated by multiplying the wavelength by the frequency:

$V = \wedge \times f$ where $\wedge$ is the wavelength and f is the frequency.

The same is true for radio waves; each wave has a wave

length and a frequency, and radio waves travel at the speed of light. Radio waves are just one type of wave from a group of waves which includes light, microwaves, and x-rays, known as electromagnetic radiation. As the word "electromagnetic" implies, all these waves have electric and magnetic parts which oscillate as they move along, and they can travel through a vacuum. This is unexpected, as waves usually need something through which to move; water waves move through water and sound waves move through air, but electromagnetic waves move through empty space and that speed is constant... it doesn't change.

So what's the difference between light waves and radio waves; we know that they're different because we can see light and not radio waves. Here's the difference between these different types of electromagnetic radiation: From our formula for speed of a wave,

$V = \wedge \times f$ where $\wedge$ is the wavelength and f is the frequency and for electromagnetic radiation, the velocity is the velocity of light. This is usually written as C, which is 186,000 miles per second. That's really fast. If you could bend light so it would travel in a circle around the earth, it would make over 7 trips in one second.

If you study that formula, you will see that if the speed is constant, then the higher the wavelength, the lower the frequency. Here's an example of how that works: if $V = 12$ and remains the same, then if $\wedge = 2$ then $f = 6$ because $2 \times 6 = 12$. But if you change $\wedge = 3$ then $f = 4$ so that $3 \times 4 = 12$. So as $\wedge$ went up, then f went down in order to keep $V = 12$. Radio waves have really long wavelengths and small frequencies and light waves have much shorter wavelengths and higher frequencies.

Here's a short trip across the electromagnetic spectrum so you can see how many different types of electromagnetic radiation there are, all made the same way and differing only in wavelength and frequency. You will see that as the wavelength decreases, the frequency increases and so does the energy of the wave. The higher the frequency the more powerful the wave.

First up are electrons traveling up and down a tall, vertical wire and producing radio waves, which have very long wavelengths and low frequencies; they're not very powerful, which is good because there are lots of them all around us all the time.

Next on the electromagnetic spectrum we'll decrease the wavelength, which will increase the frequency and we'll move into the range of microwaves. These waves are identical to radio waves in that they have electric and magnetic parts except that the wavelength is shorter and the frequency is higher, and they are more powerful. I know that you understand this as I bet you own a microwave oven.

Next in line are infra-red rays, or heat waves. With a shorter wavelength and higher frequency than microwaves, you can actually feel them in a campfire which has no more visible flame, but which emanate from the hot coals under the ashes. Put your hand out and feel the heat; that's infra-red radiation.

Moving up the spectrum (energy wise) again, we once more decrease the wavelength and increase the frequency and enter the range of visible light. White light is a mixture of all the different colors of light from red to violet; you can see this if you pass white light through a prism; the prism breaks up the white light into its colors, and you will see a rainbow with red light on one end and violet on the other with the remaining colors in between. The red light has a longer wavelength than violet and smaller frequency, which makes violet light more energetic than red light. The colors from red to violet are in order according to energy as follows: red, orange, yellow, green, blue, indigo, and violet. And the shorter the wavelength, the more bending that the color experiences as it passes through the prism.

One step past the violet light, on our journey across the electromagnetic spectrum, is ultra-violet, which is the culprit responsible for sunburn. It has shorter wavelengths and higher frequencies than the visible light and is more powerful; you found this out when you stayed out in the sun for too long a period of time. You also found that if there were a cloud covering, you still got sunburned; that's because clouds do not block ultraviolet rays. A lot of these rays are filtered out by the ozone layer in the upper atmosphere, and that's a good thing.

Shortening the wavelength once again (which increases the frequency) brings us into the realm of x-rays. These rays can go through materials, and you all have had an x-ray to diagnose health issues, either at the dentist or doctor. The technician covered the rest of your body with a lead apron to protect your body from x-rays' negative effects and then ducked for cover while they did their job. X-rays are produced when high energy electrons hit a chunk of metal and the sudden stopping takes the energy of the electron and converts it into a chunk of electromagnetic radiation-an X-ray.

One last step and we'll be done. The most powerful electromagnetic rays are gamma rays. These are produced during some types of nuclear reactions, and these are deadly. They travel through many materials, and if they hit you, they do things like change your atoms from one type into another; this is not good for your body and should be avoided.

So you've just received a short course in electromagnetic waves and how they're produced. In each case, a particle with an electric charge accelerated or oscillated and produced electromagnetic radiation. I was interested what all this had to do with experiencing God. I continued texting the Almighty.

> What do electromagnetic waves have to do with communicating with You? Are these the way to get in touch with you?

No. They're physical and I'm spiritual and even though I can sense electromagnetic waves, they're not the primary source of our communication for us. But if you understand electromagnetic radiation, it will help you imagine how spiritual waves work.

> Spiritual waves?

Sure. Remember the 3 basic quantities in nature: mass, electric charge, and spiritual substance? Well, we just talked about an electric charge can produce an electromagnetic wave. And you may have recently heard of the detection of a gravitational wave. They are very, very weak and only when huge masses, like 2 black holes, merge can detectable gravitational waves be produced.

> I just read about them. So it sounds like you're about to tell me that spiritual substance can produce spiritual waves.

Yes I am, and yes it can.

> So spiritual substance oscillates and produces waves

Sort of . . . Not exactly; but it's a good way to imagine what's going on. It's not a physical pulsation but it's a good model to use to think about what's happening.

> So, what do spiritual waves do?

There are many types of spiritual

waves from weak thought waves to intense waves of love. Just as there are many types of electromagnetic radiation in the electromagnetic spectrum, so there are all kinds of spiritual waves. There are also waves of creativity, compassion, intimacy, prayer, premonition, and other types.

> Are ideas that pop into your head due to thought waves from You or another person or are they a result of thinking with your brain?

Could be either, and you will have to practice analyzing them and observing their subtle differences. People who get good at this are usually said to have intuition.

> Do intense thought waves have higher impact on a person and thus make it easier to act on them.

Sure. Just ask all the people who canceled their 9/11 flights due to a feeling of something being not quite right. The 4 planes that crashed carried only an average of 22% of their capacity so 78% of the seats were empty.

> That's amazing. Is that list of types of spiritual waves which You gave me a complete list?

No. Almost any positive feeling associated with nature, other people, or an experience can be shared or communicated by spiritual waves. Many spiritual experiences may be a result of spiritual wave reception from Me or others.

> And love is one of the most important ones?

For sure. But not eros, the erotic love that the animal is interested in; it's agape which is spiritual.

> Are you using the Greek meanings here?

Yes. They understood it well. Agape is the deep spiritual and unconditional love which you can share with others and with Me. There's a third type, phileo, which is sort of an average of the other two. It is brotherly love, or loving others because they're worth it or deserve it.

> Does that mean that eros is a bad thing?

No, it just means that it's animal and very important for survival of the species. But for a complete and intimate sexual experience, the spirit is essential.

> But in this modern age of skimpy garments and loose morals, it's easy to lose sight of spiritual values. You know about Las Vegas, right? It keeps one perpetually horny. Are You familiar with that term.

First off, would an all-knowing God not be familiar with all words in all languages and all meanings. Your concern betrays an underlying fear that I may punish you for behaving in a way in which I made you. Remember that fear will keep you from having a relationship with me, so I encourage you to throw that fear out and keep the channels open with Me.

> I will but it's hard because I have been taught that these feelings are wrong. At one point the bible says to gouge out your eyes if looking at a babe makes you lust.

I know and it's a terrible thing. Another example of attempting to control the masses. I'm not

going to create you a certain way
and then punish you for being that
way. You just have to let your
spiritual nature channel your
animal urges.

> But it's really difficult
> sometimes. Wasn't there any
> other way to do this?

First of all, it is the animal way and
you are animal. Second of all, if you
didn't have these feelings, you might
be spending all your time fishing or
on the golf course, and because you
have an animal element in your
make-up, this pushes you toward
becoming a family man. Creating
a child is animal but then
staying around to raise your child
and becoming an important part of
your child's life is spiritual. It's a
spiritual decision, but the
animal in you got you
going. Do the prayer thing;
I can help you get through
some of these situations.

> I will. Do I have to spell it
> out or can I just think it and
> you'll get it?

You think it; I receive it.

> So what about all the fancy
> words and phrases like

> "hallowed be thy name" and "thy will be done". Don't you like those phrases.

Those are actually more for you than for Me. When you don't understand the way things work then words and phrases which you have used and which carry emotional meanings can make you more receptive and open to communication with Me.

> And since we're having thoughts all the time, then You must be tuning in to us all the time.

Yes, which means that you've got to know that I'm on your side and must learn to trust Me in every situation. If you don't, then it can drive you crazy.

> But how can you be in touch with everybody at the same time. I know you're large but that seems impossible.

You can't really understand that because you are a 3-dimensional person and I am 4-dimensional. Do you understand the 4th dimension?

> A bit, since it's a math thing.

We'll start with that tomorrow. No

psychic revelations this time; I'll
just say adieu and I'll see you then.

    And that was the end of the third day.

Chapter 4 – Thursday

I woke up thinking about the 4th dimension. A lot of the popular science programs on TV talk about different dimensions, but if you question people who watch them, they don't understand the idea well at all. To have a basic idea of this is important in the understanding of spiritual matters. If you have a good grasp of this concept, then skip the next few paragraphs.

First of all, you should know what a dimension is. Think of it as a direction. If something is one-dimensional then it must be situated on a line and it can't move off of it. Think of a truck on a straight road going east and west; the truck can go east or west but can't move north and south nor up and down. You can specify where it is located with one number; if it is 2 miles to the east of its starting point then it is at +2. If it is located 3 miles to the west of its starting point then it is at -3. One number is all that is needed to specify its location . . . one dimension. The line drawn below is a one dimensional figure. The arrowheads on the ends of the line indicate that it goes on forever . . . to infinity. The mark on the line with a zero is the starting point and the other two points mentioned above have also been noted.

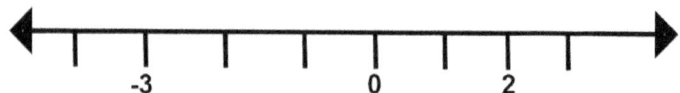

Now let's go for a boat ride on a smooth lake; it's a 2-dimensional ride. To make a 2-dimensional surface from a one dimensional line, you go to the starting point on the line and then move perpendicular to the line. Perpendicular means moving at 90°. If the line is situated in an east-west orientation, then first you would move north or go south. Here is a 3-dimensional view of a 2-dimensional surface, and if the surface is completely flat you would call the surface a plane.

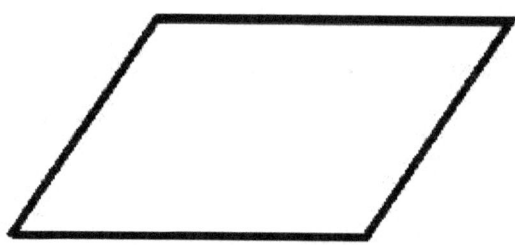

The boat can go east or west, like the truck. But now it can also go north and south. To tell where the boat is from its starting buoy, and let's use yards here, you have to say how many yards east or west it is, and then how many yards north or south. For example, if a boat goes 300 yards to the east from the starting buoy, and then turns and goes 400 yards south, you could specify its position with the 2 numbers +300 and -400, where a positive number is for east and north and a negative number is for west and south. 2 numbers . . . 2 dimensions, but it won't move up or down because that would be the third dimension. The diagram below is a picture of the location of the boat with the boat at (300,-400).

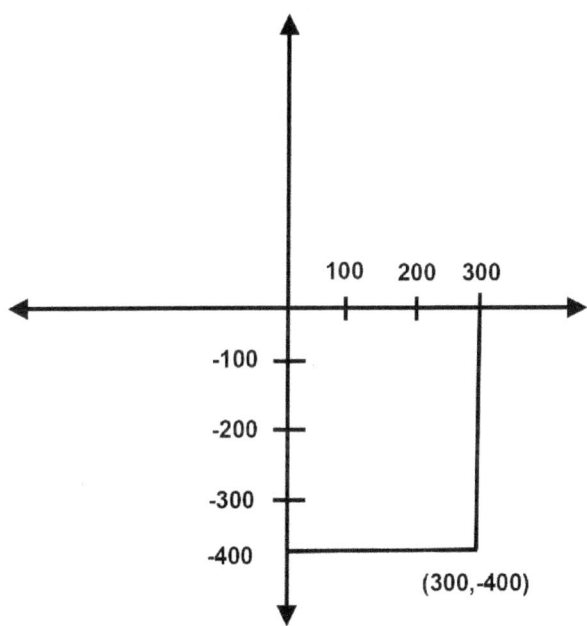

And the third dimension involves a third direction: you get to move up and down. To make a 3-dimensional space from a 2-dimensional plane, you begin at the starting buoy and move up and down making sure to keep perpendicular to both of the original dimensions. A vehicle which travels in 3-dimensions is an airplane; you specify where it is by how many miles from the airport east-west, and then how many miles north-south, and finally how many miles above the ground (negative numbers here would mean that the plane crashed). 3 numbers mean 3 dimensions. Every object you work with is 3-dimensional. Look at something in your room; it has height and width and depth. It is 3-dimensional. Here is a diagram of the plane 3 miles east of the airport and 2 miles south of the airport and 1 mile above the ground. 3 numbers are needed to specify the location of the plane, thus there are 3 dimensions.

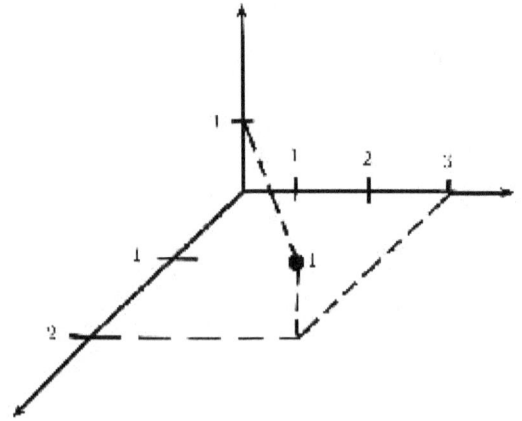

Are you ready for 4 dimensions? It is difficult to describe what the 4th dimension is and even tougher to imagine it. I can't do it, and yet I believe that it exists. Einstein showed that it does exist using mathematics, and the idea is used in advanced physics and cosmology.

I will attempt to describe it for you by going back to a 1-dimensional object, the line. How did we go from 1 to 2 dimensions? We did it by standing on the line and then moving perpendicular (that means right angles . . . 90°) to the line and the direction we moved was a new dimension. You enter a new dimension by traveling perpendicular to the old one(s).

When we were on the boat, our 2-dimensional vehicle, we then moved perpendicular to the plane, that 2-dimensional surface (like a very large sheet of completely flat paper). Large and flat and going off into 2 dimensions are the key ideas here. When we move upward off the water, then we moved into a new dimension, the 3rd dimension. Again, we moved into the 3rd dimension by moving in a direction perpendicular to our 2 dimensional plane.

Now for the 4th dimension, and it should be noted that we're not talking about time here. Often, time is considered the 4th dimension because to specify the location of an object, you should tell what the 3 numbers are to location its position in space, as well as WHEN you are stating its location. In this situation, we're talking about a 4th spatial dimension and it's difficult to imagine. But here goes. And I'm going to start abbreviating dimension with a capital D; so one-dimensional becomes 1- D and the plane is 2-D, etc.

Imagine yourself on the line (1-D) again. Now move perpendicular onto the plane (2-D) and then up perpendicular to the plane (3-D) and now . . . . . MOVE PERPENDICULAR to those 3 dimensions. Stop for a moment and think about this; see if you can visualize it.

Can you visualize that? I cannot. I can describe it and actually use math with it, but I cannot imagine it. If you can, then I admire you. I know it exists because of Einstein's General Theory of Relativity, which claims that space is curved. Because we live in 3-D space, we cannot notice it, but if space is curved, it must curve in the 4th dimension.

To see how space is curved, examine how you can curve a 2-D surface. Take out a sheet of paper and lay it flat on the table. Now lift up 2 opposite edges of the paper so it looks like the diagram below.

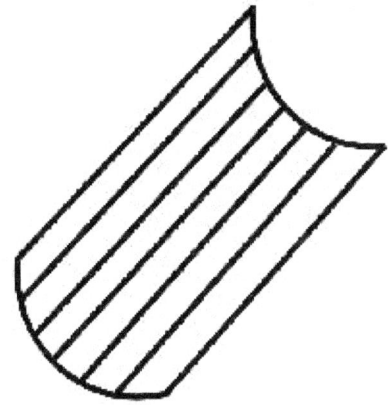

So, if a 2-D plane, is curved, it must be curved in the third dimension. Now, extend that into the next dimension; if 3-D space is curved, it must be curved in the 4th dimension. Wow! How are you doing with all of this. It's a difficult exercise, especially if you're dealing with this idea for the first time.

I can't draw a 3-D space curved in the fourth dimension, but movies and science films draw the extreme curvature of space, due to the presence of a black hole, as a whirlpool in space. The whirling center absorbs everything that gets close to it, even light, and people seem to get the idea.

So, since we have trouble imagining 4-D, how can we talk about its qualities and characteristics? The answer is by observing the behavior of a 2-D person, and thinking about it from our 3-D point of view. Then we'll extend that notion one extra dimension. Here goes.

Imagine a person who is 2-D (let's call the person JOE) and lives on a plane (that 2-dimensional flat surface). We will ignore all the problems which arise with Joe's existence and concentrate on the experience of being 2-dimensional.

Here is JOE standing on the ground.

He can only see in directions of up-and-down coupled with right-and-left. The picture shows Joe looking straight ahead (to our right). To look behind him, Joe would have to pivot his head upward, and then back down behind him (to our left). This crazy maneuver would be necessary because he is unable to look outward toward us; that is in the 3rd dimension, and he doesn't know about it and is thus unable to look in our direction. I haven't been able to figure out the anatomy of such a creature, so let's just focus on how we 3-dimensional beings relate to JOE.

Because JOE goes about his life and has no idea of a third dimension, he doesn't know that we exist. He is confined to the plane and cannot see out perpendicular to it; he cannot see us in the 3rd dimension, but we, as superior 3-D beings, are able to observe JOE without being detected or noticed, as we are in a direction which JOE cannot perceive. We can see the inside of JOE, and if we were doctors, we could do an operation without going through the skin. We could touch any organ or portion of Joe's body and harm or heal it without Joe's understanding what was going on. That was a picture of JOE with his heart visible to us but not to another 2-dimensional person. We could operate on JOE without going through his skin, and if we operated without his knowledge, he would think it was a miracle. Of course, we would use an anesthetic so it wouldn't hurt him.

Think about what JOE would see if we were to push a marble through the 2-D plane. JOE would see the following (and to imagine this you must hold up the sheet of paper and look along it like JOE would be looking): JOE would first of all see a dot and then, as the marble was pushed through, a circle starting very small and then growing bigger. After the circle became as large as it could, which is the size of the marble, then the circle would shrink back to a dot and then disappear. JOE would think it was a miraculous vision, but we would know it was just a marble going through the paper. Below are a few pictures of the marble going through the paper. The first shows the marble just touching the paper; JOE sees a dot. The second shows the marble having moved a way through the paper; JOE sees a small circle. When the marble is half way through the paper, JOE now sees a bigger circle. As the marble moves further, the circle begins to shrink and once more becomes a dot.

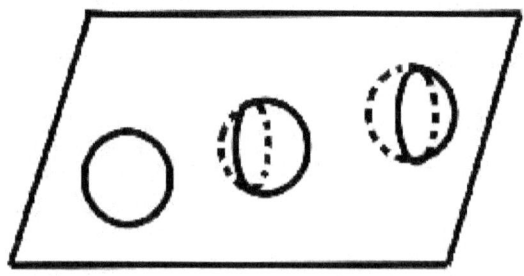

Here's another strange event. Below is a 2-D table with a

cup upside down over a ball. In order for JOE to remove the ball from under the cup, he would have to pick up the cup and grab the ball with his hand.

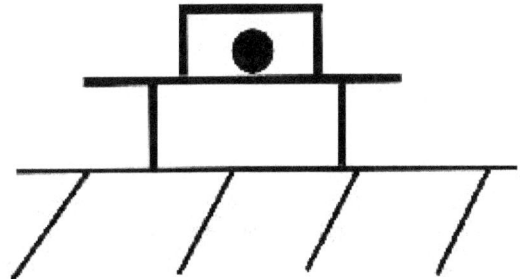

However, we 3-D beings can take the ball from under the cup by moving it out through the third dimension. We know how it disappeared, but to him, it would either be a great magic trick or a miracle.

Here's another 2-D event to consider. Below is a picture of a plane with a line in it. Points A and B are in the plane on opposite sides of the line. Because a plane is infinite, the only way to get from point A to point B, and still remain in the plane is by going through the line.

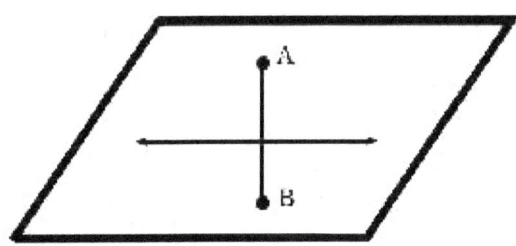

Now step up one dimension. Below is a plane which divides 3-dimensional space. Point A is on one side of the plane and point B is on the other side. I drew only a portion of the plane; please recall that a plane is infinite in both dimensions. The plane divides 3-D space into 2 parts and since the plane is infinite, then in order to go from point A to point B, you have to go through the plane.

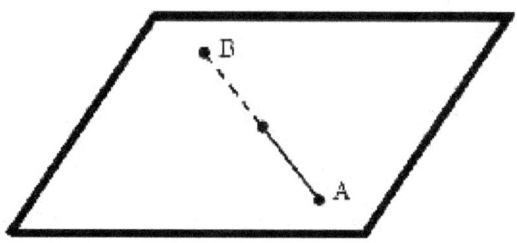

Now let's extend these examples from 3 dimensions to 4 dimensions. You are now JOE in 3-D and a 4-D being can observe you without you seeing that being because you can't look in the direction of the 4th dimension. Medical healing on your 3-D body is possible if the inside of your body is approached from the 4th dimension. Because the inside of your body is observable from the 4th dimension, then the medical problem can be solved without going through the skin.

If you place a ball on your table and put your coffee cup over it, then the ball can disappear if it is removed through the 4th dimension just like you removed the ball from under the 2-D cup by taking it out via the 3rd dimension. And a 4 dimensional hyper-sphere (that's a 4 dimensional sphere or ball), as it passes from one part of 4-D space to the other part, first appears as a dot, and then a small sphere, or ball, which then grows into a larger sphere. It then shrinks back into a small one and then disappears altogether. You can visualize this only as you go back to the marble going through the plane and try and imagine the shift upward to a 4 dimensional hyper-sphere going through our 3-dimensional space. Each one of these examples is difficult, if not impossible, to visualize, and by going back to the 2-dimensional model, you can, hopefully, imagine how these events work in 3-D space.

The last 2 examples of a line cutting a plane, and a plane cutting 3-D space, can now help you imagine what happens as our 3-D space cuts 4-dimensional space. Our 3-dimensional space will divide that 4-dimensional space into 2 parts and if you wish to travel from one part to the other, you must travel through our 3-D space. I can't draw that, so all you can do is try to imagine it as best you can. Go back to the 1-dimensional line cutting a 2-dimensional plane into 2 parts. Then move up to a 2-dimensional plane cutting our 3-dimensional space into 2 parts. Finally, move up to our

3-dimensional space cutting 4-dimensional space into 2 parts; to get from one part to the other, you must cross our 3-dimensional space.

And if we observe how much more complicated we are compared to 2-D JOE, then we can at least sense how much more complex the Almighty is, compared to us. At least I think that's where all this is going.

    I went back to texting.

> So you're a 4-D being.

Yes I am. Actually more dimensions
than that but let's just stick to the 4 and
what it means to you both now and after
you pass over.

> You mean die?

Yes, but "pass over" is a more positive
term and contains more of what actually
will happen.

> So we die and step into the
> 4th dimension.

Yes, but only the spiritual part of you.
Your physical part then decays; you
know "ashes to ashes and dust to dust"

> But we can't just step back to
> the 3rd and move around our
> old stomping grounds?

Sure, but nobody usually does. There's too much going on over here. Besides, a spiritual body doesn't do well in 3-dimensional space without being coupled to a physical being. That's why out-of-body experiences are rare in ordinary life and only those who have mastered meditation and spiritual control can perform such a task on a regular basis.

> But what if you want to go from one side of 4-dimensional space to the other?

Remember how a 2-dimensional plane separates 3-dimensional space into 2 parts.

> Yes. And to go from one part of 3-D space to the other, one must go through the plane.

You've got it. And 3-dimensional space must separate 4-dimensional space into 2 parts.

> So to go from one part of 4-D space to the other, one must go through our 3-D space. Is that right?

You understand!

> But what about the reluctance
> of a spiritual being to travel
> back into 3-D space.

Well, you should know a few things
about a spiritual being's, or soul's,
capabilities in 4-space. I won't tell
you a great deal, but I would like
to tell a few things about this place.

> Which is heaven.?

Yes but just as you can't perceive
the 4th dimension, you also can't
understand what this place is like.
There's no gender so various
expectations are dashed when
people from certain religions show up.

> What about streets of gold?

No. Sorry. But you won't care because
of the wonder and awe which you will
experience just by being here. You
can go to any part of the universe
as fast as you want and even watch stars
and galaxies form. You won't believe it.

> But to do that, you'd have to
> go to the edge of the known
> universe and since you have
> to go less than the speed of
> light that could take years to
> get there.

The speed of light limit is only for
physical 3-D objects that have a
mass measured in kg (that's kilograms)
Remember that spiritual substance is
measured in i-kilograms or i-kg. and
can travel FASTER than the speed of light.
So if you travel at a million light-years
per second, you can get to the edge of
the known universe in just under 4 hours.
That's if you measure time the same way
that you are used to; it's a little different
here, but we won't go into that now.

> Is that what makes it possible
> to go from one side of 4-D
> space to the other side
> through 3-D space?

Yes. But the other is to have a
'portal' which guides the spirit
and facilitates passage.
> How would that work?

A black hole works just fine. It provides
a tear in the fabric of space-time so that
passage is easier. And you can always
find a lot of them near the center of a galaxy.
But there are some effects that occur. Plug
in a 1 i-kg spiritual mass going at 189,700
miles per second into Einstein's relativistic
mass formula and see what you get. Do
that tonight and this'll be our starting point
for day 5. After all, there have been a lot
of very complicated ideas today and they
need time to sink in. I'll text you
tomorrow.

That sounds good.

And that was the end of day 4.

Chapter 5 - Friday

Einstein's relativistic mass equation is complicated so I'm just going to describe what it is and what it predicts. For those of you who feel adventurous and want to see how the formula works, you can see all the details in appendix A in the back of the book.

I will list Einstein's formula to start us out.

$$M_V = \frac{M_0}{\sqrt{1 - \frac{V^2}{C^2}}}$$

This formula describes what happens to a physical mass (m_0) as its speed or velocity (v) gets close to the speed of light (c). m_0 is called the rest mass of the object, which is the mass of the object when it's not moving. Once the mass starts moving, then it turns out that its new mass (m_v) is heavier than it was when it wasn't moving, and that doesn't make sense to the way we are used to viewing things; but that's the way relativity works. Note that the amount of stuff that makes up the mass has not increased; it just means that the heaviness of what's there goes up just because it's going really fast.

To see how this works, think of a rocket which blasts off from earth, except that you don't turn off the rockets when you get up to orbit altitude; you keep them on and you go faster and faster. If the rocket is providing a force to cause your acceleration to be 5 times that of earth's gravity (5g), then in order to get going just half the speed of light, you'd have to leave the rockets on for over 35 days. If you decide that you want to get going close to the speed of light, then you'll leave the rockets on for another 35 days. But when you check, you're not there yet. What's going on? Well, it turns out that no matter how long you leave the rockets on, you'll never get the rocket to go the speed of light.

Here's what's happening: as you get close to the speed of light, the energy from the rocket no longer increases the speed of the rocket. Instead, it begins to increase the mass of the rocket. I'm sure you've heard of $E = mc^2$ It usually refers to the mass lost during a nuclear reaction being changed into a large amount of energy. But, in this case, it's the reverse; the energy from the rocket is increasing the mass of the rocket. You, as a passenger in the rocket, notice nothing different from the time you began your journey, but an observer on the ground, will swear that your mass is a lot larger than when you left. Relative to the stationary observer, your mass has increased. That's the nature of relativity. And there are other things that change too, like length and time, but we'll just concentrate on mass.

Here's an example of what happens when you take a 1 kilogram mass (m_0) moving at 180,094 miles per second (v), which is almost 97% of the speed of light which is 186,000 miles per second and whose symbol is c. Plugging these values into the formula gives the result m_v = 4 kg.

This means that a 1 kg. Mass moving at 97% the speed of light will seem like it has a mass of 4 kg. So it's not 1 kg moving at 97% the speed of light; it's 4 kg moving at 97% the speed of light. This is the way the formula works with a physical mass. It doesn't have any extra mass; it's just that the mass it has now seems "heavier".

But the the assigned problem is to take an i-kg of spiritual substance and have it travel at 189,700 miles per second, which is faster than the speed of light which, we're being told, is OK for a spiritual mass to do.

Another thing never before used in this formula is an "i-mass" This seems like a difficult problem; but here we go. (remember that details are in appendix A)

$$m_0 = 1 \text{ i-kg} \quad v = 189,700 \text{ miles/sec} \quad c = 186,000 \text{ miles/sec}$$

When we plug these values into the formula, an interesting thing: happens: the denominator has an i in it. It happened that way because v was greater than c. But watch what happens now; we're going to cancel the i's . . . remember that word? It means that you have a number both in the top and bottom of the fraction and you can cross them out. Actually what you're doing is dividing a number by itself and getting 1, which doesn't alter the value of the rest of the fraction. But this time, you're canceling the i's and that's OK because they're numbers, even though they're imaginary. Doing the rest of the math gives the following result:

$$m_v = 5 \text{ kg}.$$

Now that's amazing! First of all, 1 has become 5 and instead of a spiritual substance, since there's no "i", it's a physical mass, around 11 pounds. It appears that a spiritual substance traveling just above the speed of light manifests itself as a large physical mass moving faster than the speed of light; let's report the results.

> That took some time, but I ended up with a really heavy physical mass instead of a 1 i-kg spiritual object. That's quite unexpected. How can a spiritual object change into a physical one?

Actually it doesn't change. It's still a spiritual object; it just manifests itself to its surroundings as a physical mass just as your other example had a 1 kg mass acting as if it were a 4 kg mass.

> Can one sense its presence in our 3-D space. Even though it's a 4-D object, moving through 3-D space on its way from one part of 4-space to the other.

Definitely. It's presence has been detected and scientists are baffled as to its origin.

I've heard of extra mass associated with galaxies and understood that it's that extra mass which must exist in order to explain their unusual rotation. Scientists call it Dark Matter and puzzled as to its origin.

> Is it a large effect?

With many spirits passing through
a lot of black holes, the effect becomes
quite large and, interestingly enough,
the closer to the speed of light that
you go, the larger the effective mass
becomes.

> So, as a 4-D Deity, You are
> able to be close to me, even
> though I cannot see you,
> physically, in my 3-
> dimensional space.

Yes. I'm with everyone all the time.
Since people can't imagine the 4th
dimension, they can't understand
how that's possible so they came
up with the Holy Spirit; it's actually a
good idea to help one imagine
how these kinds of things work.

> So the old idea of
> summoning You from on
> high with all kinds of
> liturgical rig-a-ma-role so
> You'll come down and
> answer our prayers is not
> right on?

Not really. As I said, those kinds of
things are more for you than they
are for Me. I'm interested in being
part of your life in many ways and
it can be a wonderful or a terrifying
thing. But remember that it is terrifying
only if you can't trust me or think

that I am out to get you. I again
say to you, "do not let fear nor
guilt nor anger keep you from Me"

> What if we want to feel
> privacy? It's hard to imagine
> someone constantly
> observing us.

I understand. Just tell Me to back off.

> How do you do that?

Thought waves and prayer waves.

> Are they different?

In wavelength and energy, but they're
all the same type of thing. You think it
I get it.

> If humans are sending waves
> and receiving waves from
> You then can we send and
> receive waves from each
> other.

Sure. But some thought waves are
pretty weak so others don't often pay
attention to them. And if they do
people often dismiss them as idle
ideas without any merit. And
when you do pay attention to them,
your brain may say "that's ridiculous"
or "that doesn't make any sense." Men

like to use logic and don't like to
make decisions based on 'feelings'.
Women are more comfortable with
this and call it 'intuition'.

> Does everyone have this
> ability?

Yes. But you have other things which
will challenge these thoughts which just
"pop into your head".

> I know one thing you
> mentioned is your brain and
> its thoughts and logic. What
> are some others?

Besides thoughts and feelings and logic
from your conscious brain, there is the
subconscious which is constantly
working and throwing thoughts into
your consciousness. Along with thoughts
from others and thoughts from Me, it's
difficult to know which is which.

> How can you know the
> difference?

Practice and experience.

> Example?

Let's say you're about to go out,
and you have the thought that you
should take your umbrella. You look
into the sky and it's clear, so you

decide not to. Then it rains. When you
look back at what happened, you
realize that you had that premonition
and paid it no attention. Next time you
can heed such information.

> What about the time that you
> get that information but then
> it doesn't rain?

Then it was probably your brain that
recalled 'the time it rained' and then
figured this was the same. That would
be a logical decision that could cloud
any spiritual input.

> And eventually I'll be able to
> tell the difference and act
> accordingly?

Yes, but you must realize that it's not
a matter of the will. You don't TRY
and force a thought from the spirit.
You STOP and be aware and wait for
that 'still small voice'. And it will
come, and you will be able to act
on it.

> It sounds like awareness is a
> key idea in becoming
> spiritual.

True. Awareness or meditation or
any technique which allows you to
become more aware or in touch with
Me.

> Why couldn't you just thrust yourself a little more emphatically into our space. That way we could experience You more "up-close" and forcefully

I don't for the same reason that a SCUBA diver uses a regulator on the air tank. If you didn't have one, the pressure from the tank would overpower the swimmer and it would be impossible to breathe with it. If you ever met Me face-to-face, I would over-whelm you and 'you would surely die'

> I get it. But are there other things I could do to get in touch with You besides 'sit and stare'?

Sure. Get out in nature.

> So, are You going to be there?

Sure, but remember that I'm also right next to you right now. We're trying the nature experience to get you to open up to Me.

> How does that help?

Three things must be considered
in order to have a situation
which is ideal for our
communication: first
we need a minimum of
residual spiritual energy from
others. It is communication
between you and Me upon
which we are focusing.

> Is that why wilderness is
> more conducive to spiritual
> awareness than, let's say, a
> group of people admiring
> Yosemite Falls?

Yes. It's like listening to a radio
station with another station
playing in the background.

> That's annoying and I can
> understand how it would
> work in a spiritual sense.

Secondly, a sublime natural setting
confounds the brain.

> Is that important?

Yes. You've seen how the brain can
introduce logical roadblocks for the
spirit, and you've got to get that out
of the way.

> By being out in nature?

Yes. When you confront situations that
overwhelm the brain's ability to take
it all in, it (the brain) sort of shuts down.
Consider the Grand Canyon. It is so large
that the brain can't handle it. The width
and depth are so tremendous that you
stand in awe. The wind is blowing and a
bird is soaring over one of the deep crevices.
You think of how long it took for it to be
formed and the length of time is impossible
to grasp. There are shapes and forms and
colors which are impossible for a human being
to mimic or become. It's an experiential koan.

> What is a koan?

It's necessary to get one's brain out of the
way so you can experience Me. The Zen
Buddhists ponder a sentence, called a
koan, which is designed to "blow your
mind". By repeating the sentence over
and over, it eventually confounds
the intellect and with your brain out
of the way, you are open to communion
with Me. The most famous one is,
"you have heard the sound of two
hands clapping; what is the sound
of one hand clapping?"

> Does that work?

Sometimes. They try too hard and they
don't listen for me to reply. But their zeal is
admirable. Experiencing the creation is

very profound and it's easy; just sit and stare. . . become aware. The rhyming makes it easy to remember that one. But don't forget that second part.

> So being out in nature eliminates other spiritual sources, moves your intellect aside, and what is the third thing?

To confront the creator, confront the creation.

> So the natural world is where you hang out a lot?

No more than anywhere else; we're talking about getting in touch and this is a good way to do so. Think about a painting that touches you profoundly. As you ponder its meaning, you also think about the painter and what he was trying to do. You think about his mind-set as he was working and his awesome ability in painting such a piece.

> I never was conscious of that, but now that You mention it, I think I understand.

And it's true for a book and its author, a building and its architect, and a symphony and its composer. To encounter the creator, experience His creation.

> Wow, I never understood why I had those feelings while standing on the ocean shore; it makes sense.

But it takes time to do it. Too often, a car pulls up to a scenic overlook, people pile out, walk around for a few minutes, then get back in and off they go. That's not a spiritual experience.

> From what You've just said, is church a good place for a spiritual experience?

It can be. When people thought that I would only show up at church then they would come to try and hook up with me there. There were some really profound spiritual experiences which occurred. It definitely is a good place for learning things and socializing with people of similar views and of pooling money to give to those in need. But too often the worship service tries to keep Me up front and at an arm's length from you, rather than encourage spiritual communion and communication with Me.

> Is it important to have others around to share these experiences?

It can be. Spiritual waves can resonate just like physical waves.

I knew what resonance was. When you have physical waves that combine, they form a more powerful wave than either of the component waves. And another example is one source of physical vibration can cause another one to begin vibrating. For example, if you have a bell that vibrates at 550 vibrations per second and you bring it close to another similar bell which is not vibrating, that second bell will begin to vibrate as it receives energy from the first bell. It sounds like spiritual waves work like that also.

Two individuals can resonate and their spiritual waves can combine with each other and with Me to produce a spiritual experience which is more powerful than either of the individual experiences are. And one individual can induce a spiritual experience in another individual in a way which is similar to the "bell" example which you gave.

Are there any down sides to the church experience?

Sure. Pooling money for the most beautiful church on the block, establishing social cliques which leave others out, and developing hateful ideas about other denominations which may not "measure up" to your social standards or doctrines are just a few.

> So churches can be good or bad?

Yes. And the worst thing that can happen is for a church or religious group to do hurt or harm to any other group in My name.

> Like anti-Semitism?

Yes. There were terrible things done to the Jews by the Christian church throughout history and then by Hitler in the holocaust. And the witch trials were as bad! And nowadays, ISIS is wreaking havoc in My Name, and they should know that there is no way that I would condone their violence. They want to kill people just because those individuals don't believe the same ideas. It's a terrible cult.

> Why such intolerance?

From an animal point of view, it's the pack mentality-you're not in our club so I want to kill you. But if you're fundamentally religious, then you want to maintain the purity of the faith, and when your image of me is the "God of Vengeance", then you want to help Me out with all these unbelievers.

> It seems that hurt and harm done in the name of religion is more brutal than someone just wanting to steal your stuff.

Yes and the conflict in Iraq still rages due to religious conflict and you remember Serbia. . . same deal. That attitude lives on. As the rule book gets thicker, the atrocities grow.

> So the solution is that everyone is your brother or sister?

Yes . . . but in a loving family.

> LOL Yes, I've seen the behavior of siblings in a crazy mixed up family.

Yep. Let's keep it loving. But tell you what: it's been quite a session. Let's wait until tomorrow to continue. Have a good sleep; I'm heading over to the Andromeda galaxy with a new group to watch a super-nova explode. They are really spectacular and these new-be's are really going to enjoy it.

And that was the end of the fifth day.

CHAPTER 6 – SATURDAY

And it was a good sleep. I woke to the sound of a text coming in and when I looked, it was a good morning greeting from Him. . . or Her. . .or. . . That confusion was the opening topic.

> Good Morning to You and I've got a question about how to refer to You, Him or Her, or It?

Makes no difference. No gender so no problem.

> But that makes me a bit uncomfortable. I grew up thinking of You as a kindly old gentleman with long hair and a beard. You know, Sistine Chapel type. It's hard to think of you in other terms.

And that's the problem. Good old Michelangelo. Great art; poor spiritual images. But back then scientific understanding was in its infancy and the earth was still flat so it was OK. The biggest problem was the original sin idea so many of his pictures go back to the Garden of Eden and try and make you feel bad because you're human.

> Yet, you described the animal part of me as having primitive instincts and urges; would that suffice as original sin?

Probably. But the church then teaches that I'm going to send you to hell if you don't seek salvation. That's really creepy; you'll go to hell because some guy ate the apple that his wife gave him. That's a terrible teaching.

> It does make it seem like You're out to get us. And yet you said to seek You out and not be afraid.

Yes. And I'm going to repeat it one more time: there is no hell. I'm not out to get you. I'm out to help you in every way live a happy, useful life. And that is my attitude toward every single human being on the face of the earth.

> So often religious teachings pit You against us; we have to conform to all the rules or else You will punish us. Now I'm hearing that it's not the case and that you're on our side.

That's right. It's not you against Me; it's you and Me against the

difficulties and problems and
challenges of life, striving to get
you to live the happiest, most
useful, most fulfilling life possible.

> But there's got to be some
> kind of punishment for the
> evil-doers. It's one of the
> things that we depend on,
> that there eventually will be
> justice for all the little guys
> who have endured all the
> crap from the rich and
> powerful.

Well, there is sort of a report card
for everyone who shows up here,
but it's not I who punishes you, it's
you punishing yourself.

> How does that work? I know
> that I'm going to go pretty
> easy on myself when it's
> my turn.

Everyone who shows up here, and
there's nowhere else to go when
you pass over, gets to go through
what I call a "Re-run"

> That sounds interesting. How
> does it work?

Everyone gets to re-run his or her
life and look at how it went.

> But a nasty person would just watch and revel in the clever, evil things that he pulled off. How is that punishment?

I didn't tell you the most important thing. As you watch your life go by, and observe the people with whom you have dealt in the course of your life, you don't just watch them, you actually experience what they went through in the situation which involved you.

> So let's cut to the extreme. Does Hitler experience the pain and fear and anguish of the Jews which were killed in the concentration camps?

Yes! Everyone of them. He gets to, or is getting to as we text, feel the pain, suffer the humiliation, experience the fear and panic not only in the actual death, but in the ghettos, the arrests, the train rides to the camps, the separation from families. Every single one! And then he gets to experience the deaths of soldiers on both sides who were fighting his terrible war and the suffering of the civilians. . . and the list goes on.

> I can see where we might almost call that a hell.

But it's of a person's own making.

Similarly, Lincoln is experiencing the joy of freedom from slavery hundreds and thousands of times while former slave owners are experiencing the whip which they themselves inflicted on the backs of so many.

> Are they aware that they're doing it to themselves?

Yes. They not only experience the event, they're also aware that they themselves are the perpetrators. They experience the pain and anguish with the knowledge that they themselves are responsible for it.

> How about the kid that is suffering while doing push-ups that the coach demands. Does the coach get to suffer that too?

Only if he's belittling or putting down the kid while he's doing it. In a case like this, the kid is there of his own volition and getting through this difficult time will help the kid grow. If he's encouraging the kid and trying to motivate then that's very positive.

> You mentioned Lincoln; will all the presidents get to experience the joy or pain of their countrymen as a result

> of their political decisions?

Certainly. With great position comes great responsibility, and when you pass laws which affect a person's life, you then get to experience the joy or pain which those laws inflict.

> Does that include going to war?

Yes. Not many wars are really valid. World War II was valid because Hitler had to be stopped. And the Civil War was also unavoidable because it was the only way to stop slavery. But going to war for an abstract ideology or economics or oil is not a good reason. But every situation is different.
The initiator or perpetrator of an unjust war will experience the soldiers' suffering as well as that of the soldiers' families.

> So neither Lincoln nor Roosevelt will experience the sufferings of those hurt by the wars.

Right.

> How about a person who doesn't step up and help someone in need and prefers to remain in the background in a state of comfort rather than help?

That's a tough one and it depends on the situation. If the person doesn't step up because of selfishness and lack of compassion, then he needs to experience the result of that involuntariness. On the other hand, if lack of participation was due to protection of one's family or other altruistic motives, then no. I judge these situations on an individual basis.

What about the CEO of a large corporation?

If the CEO of a corporation makes a decision of money over people, then he will have to experience the anguish of that his decisions have caused with his employees or the people who have born the brunt of his decisions.

Examples?

If a corporation ships jobs overseas in order to make more money for stockholders, then he will have to experience the anguish which families of his employees have experienced because of his decision. Or if an oil executive makes poor decisions about the way that tailings ponds from oil sands are handled and that results in poor health in close-by communities or it messes up the environment, then the executives must experience the the difficulties which are experienced by others. Actually, the oil-sands

projects should all be shut down; they're
terrible for the environment and the people
who live in their vicinity.

> It seems that the way you
> treat others determines the
> types of things you will
> confront in your "re-runs".

Exactly. People must realize that
everyone is their brother or sister
and must be treated with love and
compassion.

> It seems that the parable of
> the good Samaritan is the key
> to your whole message.

Good point. The rest of it all is
detail. If you love your brothers
and sisters, then rules about
stealing, killing, coveting, and
adultery all become moot.

> What about idolatry, sabbath,
> honoring mom and dad, and
> taking Your name in vain?

Idols are unnecessary; sabbath is
a good idea (everyone needs a break)
and sometimes mom and dad
don't deserve honoring,
and doing my Name is just one
of those things which the
fundamentalists like to hold up
and point to to show that

they are indeed holy.

> So you don't mind profanity?

It's no big deal. It all boils down
to attitude. A guy greeting
his friend with "how the hell
are you?" expresses love
and camaraderie and is more
caring and loving than
a dad that says to his son,
"you're really a stupid kid to
spill that glass of water. That was
dumb" No profanity there but
the hurt and bad feelings
experienced by the kid is awful.
In each case, it depends on the
amount of love and empathy shown
by those involved.

> So the only thing we should
> worry about is how we treat
> others?

Sure. And how you treat the
environment. But the way you
treat the environment is actually
how you treat others because
people live in the environment.
So honoring the environment
honors the people who live there,
both locally and globally.

> But it's difficult to treat
> others nicely when they've
> been treating you poorly.

You've got to deal with others on a spiritual level rather that an animal level. Send out spiritual waves of love to those with whom you have a problem.

> That's hard to do.

I know, but here's an interesting thing that happens. When you send out a wave of love or joy or happiness to someone, you get an amount which "kicks back" to you. It's like the recoil of a shotgun when you're shooting at a target; the b-b's go toward the target and the gun recoils and smacks you in the shoulder. It works that way with spiritual waves also.

> That sounds like Newton's 3rd law; you know, "for every action, there's an equal and opposite reaction."

Yes. It works that way in the spiritual realm also. You send out a wave of happiness or love toward another person and an equal amount recoils back to you... which means that you just got back that which you sent out. It costs you nothing and you'll probably get back a wave from that person, which increases your spiritual energy. Are you familiar with the way a photon energizes an atom?

Yes I am.

I understood the idea well. A photon is a chunk or particle of light. I know, in past chapters I talked about the way light is an electromagnetic WAVE and now I'm saying it comes in chunks or particles. You're asking how can something be a wave and a particle at the same time. Well, it's another one of those ideas which is difficult to imagine but is well accepted in the world of physics and specifically in Quantum Mechanics. You won't be able to observe the wave nature of a baseball in flight; it's too big and the wave-particle duality of matter only becomes important with very small objects like electrons and photons.

In order to understand how a photon can energize an atom, you have to understand that the electrons which move around the nucleus of an atom are situated in certain places or locations called orbitals. Each electron, in its orbital, has a certain amount of energy and in order for an electron to move from one orbital to a different one, it must absorb enough energy to make that move.

Think of yourself on a ladder; you can be only on one of the rungs and in order to move from one rung to the next, you must gain the energy to do so. So you are the electron, the rung is the orbital, and the energy which is necessary to move from one rung to the next is the photon.

The thing about atoms is that as soon as the electron moves up to a higher energy level, it will immediately drop back down to its original energy level and when it does, it releases an amount of energy as a photon.

You can observe this for yourself by taking a fork, getting the prongs wet with water, and then putting salt on the wet tip. Now turn on the gas burner on your kitchen stove. Hold the salty fork tip in the flame, being careful not to burn yourself. You will see an orange-yellow flame being produced.

Salt is a compound made of sodium and chlorine atoms and they are absorbing energy from the gas flame and with increased energy, the electrons are moving up to a higher energy level. But electrons like to have the lowest energy possible so they immediately drop back down to a lower energy orbital, and, in doing so, emit a photon of light of a certain color and energy . . . orange-yellow for sodium. There are formulas which allow you to calculate what color of light corresponds to what energy and each atom has its own unique variety of colors which it produces.

So much for a 5 minute lesson in atomic theory. I texted back:

> Does a spiritual wave act like a photon.

Yes it does, with a few differences.

> What happens?

Just like with photons and atoms, a spiritual wave energizes a person's spirit. I'm sure you've experienced this.

> I sure have. Another person can make you happy just being around them; a person can smile at you and you'll feel happier because of that experience. Does the energy stay with you?

It all depends. Like the atom, the energy can radiate away. But unlike the atom, spiritual energy can linger and does not dissipate immediately.

> What determines how long it remains?

Some substances glow in the dark. This means that the energy which they absorbed from light during the day is slowly emitted by the atoms over time. Spiritual energy can dissipate over time or it can linger over a long period of time . . . depending on . . . wait for it. . . the WILL. There it is again; a person's 'will' determines to a great extent, how long you keep that positive energy. A person <u>decides</u> to be happy, caring, loving, and the myriad of other positive spiritual qualities, or decides to be angry and bitter.

But it's hard to live with a positive attitude when you are in a difficult situation like poverty or sickness.

Yes it is. That's why you need to experience positive spiritual energy to elevate your spirit. Energizing experiences can be provoked by being in nature, or experiencing music, literature, poetry, or other artsy types of things. Positive spiritual waves from any source, be it from Me or other people are also important. Plus, as your brain begins to realize the true happiness which results from spiritual experiences, it'll begin letting the spirit, rather than the animal, run the show.

> But when a person is born into poverty, it's difficult to become positive as you struggle just to survive.

True. That's why it's so important for everyone to love others as your brother and sister. Love from others is sometimes the key for a person to take the steps necessary to improving their situation.

> As well as physical assistance?

Yes. Assistance from individuals, churches, charitable organizations, and government programs are all valuable in helping those in need. But once a person has their basic needs met, their happiness is their decision.

> So shopping is not the key to happiness?

Nope. Once you buy your stuff, it'll satisfy you for a while, but you then tire of it (hedonistic adaptation) and have to go out and buy more stuff.

> Sounds like an addict mentality.

Yes. Only the rich understand that money doesn't buy happiness.

> But they also say that being rich is better than being poor.

The key is to have everybody at a level where they don't have to worry about want or security. That's difficult to do because rich individuals want it all. They would rather increase their dividends and profits rather than granting those who work for them a living wage.

> So the story of the rich getting into the kingdom of heaven having the same chance as a camel going through the eye of a needle is accurate?

Pretty much. The greedier you become, the more you are influenced by your animal and the less spiritual you are. It's a vicious circle.

> It seems that the more spiritual you are, the more you are willing to share and consider others as brothers and sisters.

Yes. And to break out of

greed and self-centeredness
you've got to seek the
spiritual by the means we've
discussed.

> And prayer?

Yes. But you've got to
remember how I answer
prayer; too many people
who feel that they're "holy"
think that if they say the
magic words, then poof,
they get whatever they
ask for.

> Magic words?

Yes. "In Jesus name" When
the fundamentalists pray, then
they think that if they say this,
then I will grant them what
they want.

> Isn't it in the Bible?

Yes, but they miss the meaning.

> Which is?

Jesus had all these spiritual ideas
down pat, so when you pray in his
name, you mean that the answer
to the prayer should be in harmony
with his nature. That means it
should include everybody.

> I'm not sure what You mean.

Well, I will not answer a prayer which is not to everyones' benefit. If a possible answer to a prayer harms or hinders anyone at all, then the answer is either "no" or else it's some modification of the original prayer.

> Example?

Probably the most obvious one is a player on a team praying for victory. I'll answer a players request to do his best, but I won't cause the one team to win over another.

> So when a player scores a touchdown and kneels in obvious gratitude to You, he'd better be thanking You for Your help in energizing him to do his best?

Yes. Because I didn't make him score; he _did_ it because _he_ did it. Perhaps our talk made him discard inhibitions or maybe his increased confidence made him go the extra mile, but _he_ did it.

> I guess it wouldn't work very well when both teams pray

>   for victory.

You can see the problem can't you?
Guess what! It's quitting time and
your grandkids want to go out to eat.

>   Sounds good to me. I'm glad
>   we've had this time together.
>   I can now go out to eat and
>   leave an empty chair to help
>   me imagine that You are
>   present with us.

And all I need in the way of an invite
is merely a thought from you.

>   I sure wish that the church
>   would advertise this way of
>   communicating with you; it's
>   very neat.

It's another power play from
the church. They made it known
long ago that I am done revealing
myself directly to people; instead,
they must go through the bible and
the church rather than do the kind
of thing we're doing.

>   I will do my best to get the
>   word out about direct
>   communication with You
>   and will describe all the
>   things you've taught me.

Good. Tomorrow then.

And that was the end of the sixth day.

Chapter 7 – Sunday

I woke up with great anticipation of the new ideas I could learn from texting the Almighty today and when communication was established, I received the message:

Well, this is our last day to text
like this.

That put a damper on my enthusiasm, and I expressed that thought:

>Oh, no! I love
>communicating
>like this. Why must it stop?

Oh, it doesn't have to stop. We just
won't be using the phones; actually,
I'm not using one anyway.

>Wow! How does that work?

Don't ask. It's been a great
departure from the way I
usually do things. We'll just
go back to prayer waves that
we previously discussed.

>I feel honored to have been
>able to do this with You.

I'm glad. But now the real work

begins for you.

> What do You want me to do?

Write down the things that we've discussed and get them out there for others to read and hopefully understand.

> Shall I try and start a new church?

No! Churches are divisive and there are too many of them out there anyway. And many of them are playing the "everyone in our church is right and the rest of you are wrong!" game. Churches are not bad per se. For some people, it's the only place where I get to greet them. It can be a wonderful place for people to come together and hang out with Me. Many churches do some great things in My Name and that shouldn't stop. Encourage people from different churches to come together.

> So, stress the fact that everyone is your brother or sister?

Yes, that's very important. Remember "people over principle" You don't stop loving a brother or sister because a rule was broken. And if they do things that anger you,

then talk to them and send those
waves of prayer and love.

> Another question which I've
> wondered about: What's
> more important, to enjoy
> life or to help others?

It's important to enjoy life. Everyone
has been given a great gift: life.
So enjoy it and share that joy with
others. Those are two big items
to stress. Which is more important?
Well, you shouldn't just do one of them.
If you just enjoy everything, then you
become selfish; if you just concentrate
on others in need all the time, it'll
drive you nuts because of the anguish
you'll feel over the inequality that is
causing these people to be in need.

> So somewhere in the
> middle?

Yep and it's your call. You'll find that
to really enjoy life, you've got to
be enjoying it with someone, be it
family or friends. And if you really
like helping others, you'll be enjoying
life; it's a win-win situation.

> And do something
> worthwhile?

Yes. And consider others when
deciding what you want to do with

your life. Remember the "re-run"
and vow to enjoy yourself as you're
being experienced by others during
your "re-run"

> How about money; should
> I try and make a lot of it?

Money, per se, is not a bad thing.
The Bible does not say that money
is the root of all evil; it says that the
LOVE of money is the root of all evil
That's a big difference. Money can
help you enjoy life and help a lot of
people in need, but a lot of it
belonging to a single person seems
to create selfishness and greed.

> So the goal is to help
> others so that there's no
> more poverty in the world?

Yes, but that's a big order and so
far it hasn't happened. Think of
money as manure: pile it up in a
pile for one person and it begins
to stink; spread it around and it
helps things grow.

> How do we determine our
> life's purpose? Will You tell
> us?

No. You call it. But I can sure
help you do some planning. All
you've got to do is get in touch

with Me; and I've told you how
to do that, remember?

> Yes I do. 1) sit and stare
> and be aware, then
> 2) think a prayer and
> 3) wait for Your response
> and 4) practice so you can
> differentiate between
> You, waves from other
> people, your mind, and
> your subconscious.

Seems pretty simple, eh?

> It does. I wish more
> people would talk with you
> like this?

They don't think they can, and, as
I mentioned a couple times
during our texting, they're feeling
afraid of Me, guilty, or angry at Me,
and that keeps them from
approaching Me. This is why
you've got to inform them
that it is possible. Plus, they don't
spend much time with the "sit and
stare" part. When you've got TV
and the internet and smart-phones, you
never have any alone time.

> Could it be that they don't
> believe that You exist?

Of course.

> How do you answer a belief like that? What if the waves we're getting aren't from You, but are from others or our brain or our subconscious? How can we tell the difference?

Sometimes you can't. Only with belief plus practice plus experience will you be able to differentiate between them.

> If we can't tell the difference, then how do we know it's You. One could argue that it questions your existence.

I know it does. But even if I don't exist, wave transference of thoughts, feelings, and love among people and becoming aware of the output from your brain and subconscious is a good thing. It will help average people in their lives both in direction and satisfaction. But I do exist, so the comment is moot.

> Well, I'll do my best. Please keep an eye on me and let me know of any new things to include in my book.

I will. This has been different for Me. I've enjoyed it and look forward to continuing our talk via spiritual waves and messages.

Yes. Thank You.

I then sent the last message and that was it.

Finis

There have been 7 days of texting the Almighty, and try as I may, I have not been able to reconnect with Him, or Her, or It since then. The Bible said God rested on the 7th day, so I felt honored that I was able to text during the 7th day of this week of texting, and had not received a message of "not available. . . day of rest!" With a certain amount of sadness, I accepted the fact that the whole experience was finally over, and that I was on my own. Well, not really. . . it's just different from picking up my phone and texting. I found myself eager if see if prayer thoughts as spiritual waves would actually work.

I found a quiet place and sat and stared and then thought, "You there Lord?". Then I waited; I felt a sense of what I thought was His presence and a thought popped into my consciousness, "Yes I am. See, this is OK."
I'm a doubter and wondered if it could be my brain or my subconscious. I thought, "How can I be sure that this is real?"

I immediately got back the impulse, "You can't. But give it a chance; it takes time." And I knew it would.

After several weeks of practicing the sending of prayer thoughts to Him and others and then sensing their replies, I feel that my ability has improved. I find that sometimes my thoughts go so fast that I lose my chain of thought. Sometimes, I say the prayer in words, and that lets me focus my thoughts. It seems that I'm in constant contact with Him with thought prayers like "That is great pizza Lord", "My wife is in a crazy mood today; You've gotta give me a hand with her.", "It'd be great if You could help me find a parking place.", "It'd be nice if the rain would hold off until I'm finished raking the leaves.", "Wow, that's a great sunset!", and "I really need help finding a birthday present for my daughter."

    The pizza was a thank you thought prayer, as was the sunset. I did find a parking place right away and I found a great gift for my daughter. The rain did not hold off, but I had the distinct impression that someone else needed it more than I disliked it. As a result, I went inside and saw a TV show which I didn't know was on, and which I had hoped to watch sometime; maybe that was the positive spin on the rain thing. And when I waited for a response from my "give me a hand" request, I had a distinct feeling that
He was giving me some spiritual applause! And they say that the God doesn't have a sense of humor.

    I continue to grow and am getting used to an almost new way of life. I wrote down all the texts which came in, and the book you've just read is the result. I wish you the best with these new ideas, and feel confident that the techniques which you are developing will give you a satisfying, useful, and joyful life.

Appendix

This appendix contains the calculations which produced the values of the mass which were displayed in chapter 5. That equation is a little complicated, but since you're here, I bet you feel somewhat adventurous, and will try and follow the calculations. I'll assume you know little about math, like I did with "i", and see if I can make some sense out of it for you.

A formula is like a recipe using symbols; do what it says and you'll get results. For example, if you're going to put carpeting in your living room, you'll have to know how many square feet there are. In the formula for area of a rectangle, A=lw or area = length times width. You have to know that l stands for length and w stands for width and when you put 2 letters next to each other, it means multiply them together. . . math code.

Einstein's formula is a little more complicated and describes what happens to a physical mass as it goes faster and faster. As it approaches the speed of light, its mass increases, and that's weird because it doesn't mean that the amount of stuff goes up; it just means that the heaviness of what's there goes up, just because it's going close to the speed of light. Here it is

$$M_v = \frac{M_0}{\sqrt{1 - \frac{v^2}{c^2}}}$$

Here's a verbal statement of what this formula says:

1) Take the rest mass (that's m_0 and is the mass of the object when it's not moving) and then

2) divide it by the denominator, which is calculated in the following way:

    a) take the velocity, v, of the mass, which is the speed of the mass, and square it (multiply it by itself).

    b) Divide that by the square of the speed of light, which is the square of 186,000.

    c) Take that result and subtract it from 1

    d) then take the square root.

After you divide the rest mass by the denominator, you get the apparent mass of the object. This is the mass which the object seems to have as it is moving at that speed.

Here's an example of what happens when you take a 1 kilogram mass (2.2 lb) moving at 180,094 miles per second, which is almost 97% of the speed of light.

First square 180,094 (that's 180,094x180,094); you get 32,434,000,000. (rounded off to 5 places)

Then square 186,000; 186,000x186x000 = 34,596,000,000.

Now divide the first number by the second to get 0.9375

Plugging this into the formula gives the following:

$$M_V = \frac{M_0}{\sqrt{1 - 0.9375}}$$

Doing the subtraction and square root yields

$$M_V = \frac{M_0}{\sqrt{0.0625}} = \frac{1 \text{ Kg}}{0.25}$$

Now plug in the mass of 1 kg. and divide by 0.25 and you get

$$m_V = 4 \text{ kg}$$

This means that a 1 kg. Mass moving at 97% the speed of light will seem like it has a mass of 4 kg. So it's not 1 kg moving at 97% the speed of light; it's 4 kg moving at 97% the speed of light. This is the way the formula works with a physical mass. It doesn't have any extra mass; it's just that the mass it has now seems "heavier".

The next problem is to take an i-kg of spiritual substance and have it travel at 189,700 miles per second. This is faster than the speed of light which, we're being told, is OK for a spiritual mass to do.

Another thing never before used in this formula is an "i-mass" This seems like a difficult problem; but here we go.

$$M_V = \frac{M_0}{\sqrt{1 - \frac{V^2}{C^2}}}$$

V = 189,700 miles/sec M_0 = 1 i-kg

Remember the routine: first square 189,700 and get 35,986,090,000.

Then square 186,000, which we already know is 34,596,000,000.

Then divide 35,986,090,000 by 34,596,000,000 = 1.04. Plugging this into the formula gives

$$M_V = \frac{1 \text{ i-kg}}{\sqrt{1 - 1.04}} = \frac{1 \text{ i-kg}}{\sqrt{-0.04}}$$

Oh-oh, there's that minus sign inside the square root; but from our study of "i", we know how to handle that:

split -.04 into (-1) x .04

Then $\sqrt{.04} = 0.2$ and $\sqrt{-1} = i$

Plugging these into the formula gives

$$M_v = \frac{1 \text{ i-kg}}{0.2i}$$

Now we're going to cancel the i's ... remember that word? It means that you have a number that you're multiplying in both the top and bottom of the fraction, and you can cross them out. Actually what you're doing is dividing a number by itself and getting 1, which doesn't alter the value of the rest of the fraction. But this time, you're canceling the i's and that's OK because they're numbers, even though they're imaginary.

Finally, divide 1 by 0.2 to get the following result:

$$m_v = 5 \text{ kg}.$$

This means that 1 i-kg of spiritual substance going at a

speed of 189,700 miles per second will behave like a 5 kilogram physical mass going that fast.

www.ingramcontent.com/pod-product-compliance
Lightning Source LLC
Chambersburg PA
CBHW071631080526
44588CB00010B/1366